SEASONS
OF
Prayer

SEASONS OF *Prayer*

Rediscovering Classic Prayers Through the Christian Calendar

DONNA FLETCHER CROW

Beacon Hill Press of Kansas City
Kansas City, Missouri

ISBN 083-411-8718
Printed in the
United States of America

Cover Design by Ted Ferguson

Unless otherwise indicated, Scripture quotations are from the King James Version.

Permission to quote from the following translation of the Bible is gratefully acknowledged: From the *New King James Version* (NKJV). Copyright © 1979, 1980, 1982 Thomas Nelson, Inc.

Library of Congress Cataloging-in-Publication Data

Crow, Donna Fletcher.
    Seasons of prayer : rediscovering classic prayers through the Christian calendar / Donna Fletcher Crow.
        p. cm.
    Includes bibliographical references.
    ISBN 0-8341-1871-8
    1. Church year—Prayer-books and devotions—English. 2. Prayer—Christianity. I. Title.
    BV30 .C76 2000
    242'.3—dc21   99-058765

10   9   8   7   6   5   4   3   2   1

For
Thomas Fletcher Crow
May he grow up to be a man of prayer

Contents

Foreword

LIVING BY THE CHRISTIAN CALENDAR

The Ten Commandments tell us to remember the Sabbath day to keep it holy. If we are to be totally committed to the will of God, however, we must remember the Sabbath year and keep it holy. All of time is God's. All should be kept holy.

Keeping time by the Christian calendar helps us live in the gospel. To follow the Christian calendar is to live every day in relationship to the life of Christ as He lived it on earth. To observe the passage of each year by remembering and walking through Christ's ministry on earth is in a small way to live our days here as He lived them.

We live "cumbered about much serving . . . and troubled about many things" as Christ told Martha, yet our souls long for that good and needful part that Mary chose. By following the Christian year we can have the best of both worlds, so to speak. That is, we can have both aspects of the spiritual world if we break free from trying to live Christian lives in a world that marches to a different calendar. We can be both Mary and Martha if we truly learn to be Mary first. If we can free ourselves of worldly pressures enough to spend time sitting at His feet in contemplative prayer, clear our minds enough to practice His presence wherever we are, take time to read His Word like a conversation with a dear friend, rather than a teeth-gritting study—if we can love with Mary, then we can go out and serve with Martha.

We all have to be freed of time compulsions if we are going to be freed of the frenzies and pressures of popular culture. And only when we have this freedom can we truly commit all our time to Him, to go forth in His strength to serve our world.

For many, even for lifelong Christians, this will be entirely new—a new way of keeping time and a new way of praying. Much of this book is revolutionarily new—precisely because it is so old. This is how Christians have been praying and keeping time since New Testament days, but, like so much else, in the rush of our hurried lives these classic approaches to God have fallen by the wayside. There is no better time to rediscover the classics than now.

As we pack our bags to enter a new millennium, we must fill them with the best of the old in order to face the new. We need the wisdom and strength of those who have gone before us in order to build for the future.

Introduction

Seasons of Prayer is an in-depth study and personal application of selected prayers from the Old and New Testaments and from those prayers Christians have prayed for hundreds of years. Use the study to deepen your prayer life and to increase your understanding of our spiritual heritage. For each of the classic prayers we look at its history, its use through the ages, and its theological content. Then we explore ways of making the prayer even more meaningful through personal application in our daily devotional lives.

JOURNALING YOUR PRAYER LIFE

These are prayers that grow in their significance with repeated use. Their deep meanings come alive in our daily lives through meditating on them and applying them to the situations we face each day. Besides the workbook space provided here for individual devotional study, each person should keep his or her own prayer journal as well. If you're not already accustomed to doing so, you will be amazed at how meaningful this will become to your devotional life. Writing out your prayer list will keep your mind from wandering and serve as a reminder to say "Thank You!" for answered prayers. And writing out your prayers can be an illuminating experience as it will seem that your pen finds words your mind has never thought.

I've kept a journal since I was in grade school. In those days we called them diaries and used those pages to divulge the passions and deepest secrets of our love lives. And, come to think of it, that's just exactly what you'll be doing in your prayer journal—writing down the names of the people dearest to you, jotting down the longings of your heart, writing love letters to your Supreme Lover, Jesus Christ, and recording His answers.

I recently took a few minutes to look back through my journal and found pretty much what one would expect: accounts of days of delight and days of drudgery; lists of people and situations to pray for (and lists of answers!); jottings of important Bible verses; and gaps in the dates that indicate periods of simply holding steady with "routine" praying without any fresh inspirations that I rushed to record. And I found some things I want to mention to you because you might not think of recording them in your journal, but they were some of the most meaningful to look back on: poems and prayers I had written for people or situations; accounts of images that had come to my mind as I prayed for specific needs; a little story I had written out and then asked myself, "Where did that come from?" as I reread it; I had even pasted in pictures of people and places to pray for. And I found classic prayers from the Bible and prayer books that I had copied and then rewritten to apply to situations in my own life—just as we'll be doing as we work through this book.

So let your journal be more than just a place for the answers to these chapter questions, let it be a repository of needs and delights, a creative tool to help you become a more useful tool in the Maker's hand.

THE CHRISTIAN CALENDAR

This study is organized around the church year. Although the study can be undertaken at any time and the prayers used throughout the year, I believe that you will find that entwining the rhythms of your prayer life with the rhythms of the year, alternating times of rest and preparation with times of growth, highlighted with the great festivals, will help make prayer as natural a part of our lives as the changing of the seasons.

Although the church year actually starts with Advent—preparing for the birth of Christ—I have chosen to begin this study with Lent— preparing for Easter. My reasons are twofold: First, most people are accustomed to thinking in terms of the secular calendar, so it will seem more natural to undertake a new study shortly after the new secular year begins—perhaps something like making a New Year's resolution. Second, for almost 2,000 years Lent has been the time of deepest introspection for Christians and the time most naturally given to taking on a new spiritual journey—such as studying these new approaches to old prayers. So I invite you to come on this exciting journey with me.

OVERVIEW OF THE CHURCH YEAR

Do you remember the classic William Dean Howells story "Christmas Every Day"? I loved it as a child. I was especially fascinated by the father's account of the Fourth of July: Fireworks turned into raisins and sugarplums, and several men were injured when a cannon turned into bits of rock candy and exploded—all because the little girl had wished every day could be Christmas.

"That's just too much of a good thing," my daddy would say. Our Creator knows we can handle only so much feasting. Just like the God-ordained cycle for seeds of resting, planting, growing, and harvesting, so people need the cycle of seasons for spiritual growth. God knew His creatures well when He established this pattern alternating rest and celebration. Human beings need structure, we need events to mark the passage of our days—things to look forward to in anticipation and to look back on with joy. But, just like William Dean Howells's little girl, we can't live forever in a feasting mode. God knew Christmas and the other feasts of His Church would mean more to us if separated by periods of preparation, self-examination, and ordinary growth.

Following the Christian calendar is really a whole different way of keeping track of time. It is living every day in relationship to the life of Christ as He lived it on earth. To observe the passage of each year by remembering and walking through Christ's ministry on earth is in a small way to live our days here as He lived them. Following the Christian calendar is an acting out of Christ's ministry on earth.

Recently a friend, a devout Christian and lifelong church member asked me, "Why should we observe the Christian calendar?" Perhaps many of you who have been Christians all your lives without bothering about such things are wondering the same thing.

In recent years interest in observing Lent and Advent and other events in the Christian year have undergone a tremendous upsurge of interest. Why? I haven't read any scholarly studies on the subject, but I strongly suspect that the noise and rush of modern life has driven many people to feel the need, as Dr. John E. Riley was fond of advising his college students, to "slow down and let your soul catch up with you."

In *Worship Old and New* Robert Webber says that there are good reasons to restore the Christian year. It is "rooted in the biblical and historical tradition of worship"[1] and in following the Christian year we are "remaining faithful to the Christian tradition."[2] Observing the Christian year contrasts us to the secular community. "Time in the Christian church is governed by the life, death, and resurrection of Jesus Christ, not civil or national holidays."[3]

As we study this book we will walk and pray through six Christian seasons:

1. Lent is the deepest season of self-examination and self-denial, preparing us to enter vicariously into the experience of Christ's death. It begins with Ash Wednesday, lasts for six and a half weeks—40 days excluding Sundays—and ends on Palm Sunday, which ushers in Holy Week.

2. Holy Week includes five commemorations: Palm Sunday, recalling the day of Jesus' triumphal entry into Jerusalem when the crowd proclaimed Him as the Christ; Maundy Thursday, when the Lord instituted His Supper and we remember Christ's washing of His disciples feet to emphasize the importance of service and almsgiving; Good Friday, when the sacrificial death of Christ is reenacted in many churches by stripping the altar, wearing black, and meditating on Christ's journey to the Cross; and Holy Saturday, a time of waiting that ends in the triumphant joy of Easter Sunday (beginning at sundown Saturday) when traditionally candles are once again lit in the churches, bells rung, and alleluias! proclaimed.

3. Pentecost is the birthday of the Church and marks the coming of the Holy Spirit into the world. Because of its special emphasis on holi-

ness and its application to the individual believer, this feast day should be given far more significance than it often is. Traditionally altars are draped in red and worshipers join in the festival by wearing the celebratory color, which also reminds us of Christ's blood shed for us and the blood of the martyrs.

4. Ordinary time, symbolized by the color green, is the time for growth and for focusing on the life of the Church. Many churches today are calling this season Kingdomtide, as we grow in the Church and build the Kingdom. As you observe the Church calendar, you will notice that approximately half of the year focuses on the life of Christ and half on the life of the Church. Kingdomtide, or ordinary time, is the season for building the Body of Believers.

5. And then the Church calendar, as well as the secular calendar, returns to preparation for a great festival. The Church year really starts with Advent—the preparation for celebrating the coming of Christ into our world and the Church's looking forward to His second coming. Once again many church altars are draped in purple to remind us we must be in mourning for our sins and the sins of the world, as well as in a state of anticipation, saying, "Come, O come, Emmanuel, set thy captive people free," as we prepare for the coming of the King of Kings.

6. The four weeks of Advent culminate in the joy of Christmas when the altars are once again draped in white, often with trimmings of gold and red as well. In medieval times Christmas was celebrated for 12 days (just like in the familiar carol) beginning on December 25 and ending January 6. Traditionally, all the people of a manor would gather in the great houses for times of feasting accompanied by music, plays, and assorted amusements such as jugglers and trained bear acts; while in the churches every service was a celebration of the birth of Christ.

And it all concluded in Twelfth Night, or Epiphany, which again had its secular and sacred applications—just as do our Christmas celebrations today. Shakespeare's play *Twelfth Night* was written for this occasion in London's Inns of Court while the churches proclaimed a festival of light for "the Light that had come into the world to light every man to salvation." Many churches still hold Epiphany services on or near January 6. The word *Epiphany* actually means "manifestation." Because Christ is manifest in our world and in our lives, we celebrate and praise, we study and pray that we may grow more like Him and shed His light abroad.

We will look at each season in more depth as we undertake our prayer adventure. It is my prayer that as we choose to walk in Jesus' footsteps through His earthly journey we may come to understand more of Him, become more like Him, and be able to communicate Him better to our world.

PART I

Praying

the Lord's Prayer
Through Lent

The Lord's Prayer

Our Father which art in heaven,
Hallowed be thy name.
Thy kingdom come.
Thy will be done
in earth, as it is in heaven.
Give us this day our daily bread.
And forgive us our trespasses,
as we forgive those who trespass against us.
And lead us not into temptation,
but deliver us from evil:
For thine is the kingdom, and the power, and
    the glory, for ever.
Amen.

—Matt. 6:9-13
Adapted from the KJV

Ash Wednesday: A Time for Petition and Repentance

We were just a little uneasy. We had never done this before. We knelt at the altar as the minister prayed, "Almighty God, You have created us out of the dust of the earth: Grant that these ashes may be to us a sign of our mortality and penitence, that we may remember that it is only by Your gracious gift that we are given everlasting life; through Jesus Christ, our Savior."

"Amen," we responded as Pastor Brian dipped his thumb in a small bowl of ashes and marked a smudgy black cross on each forehead.

Back in the car my daughter looked in the mirror, "Ooh," disappointment rang in her voice. "It hardly shows. I wanted a nice dark one so it'd last all day." She was going back to school. My husband, who had an appointment with his banker, pulled a handkerchief from his pocket and gave his forehead a good scrubbing. I was headed back to my computer, which was unlikely to note whether I had marked the beginning of the Lenten season by attending an Ash Wednesday service.

But in my heart I was very glad I had, because this year I was going to "do" Lent. Since childhood I had been frustrated by the way Easter seemed to sneak up on me without warning. I was never really ready to celebrate the glories of the day. And the feeling had increased through the stages of motherhood as sometime in the week before Easter I would suddenly realize, Help, we have to dye eggs and make baskets! I have to plan a dinner! The kids need new clothes! And the years I was involved in a pageant at church were worse yet—I didn't even have time to get upset over not having enough time.

Somehow, the early Christians seem to have handled things better. Maybe we can learn from them. They started six and a half weeks before Easter—examining and simplifying their lives and preparing their hearts for the greatest of all Christian festivals. And they began by observing Ash Wednesday. This observance is a very ancient tradition. The earliest detailed account of Lenten ceremonies is in the *Apostolic Tradition of Hippolytus*, written around the year A.D. 200.

It was the practice in Rome for new Christians to begin a period of public penance on that day. They dressed in sackcloth and remained apart from social contact until they were reconciled with the Christian community on Maundy Thursday (the Thursday before Easter). In the sixth century Pope Gregory I (who also developed the Gregorian chant) added sprinkling the penitents with ashes, which gave the day the name Ash Wednesday.

When the practice of public repentance fell into disuse sometime in the eighth century, the beginning of Lent was marked by a service that included the recitation of seven penitential psalms and the placing of ashes on the heads of the entire congregation, accompanied by the traditional words, "Remember, O man, that you are ashes, and to ashes you shall return" (see Gen. 3:19).

Today many churches hold similar services, such as the one my family attended, where the worshiper receives a cross marked on the forehead with the ashes obtained by burning the palms used on Palm Sunday the year before. Some people find that wearing purple clothing items (a traditional color of mourning) helps them focus on the season. Last year my daughter added beauty to our season by planting in our garden a Lenten rose, a lovely purple flower that blooms in February—even in Idaho!

Through the ages the day has been kept in various ways. You will soon notice that I have a passion for history. I love knowing about people in past times—how they lived, what they said, what they thought, how they worshiped. One of the very best ways to learn these things is by reading the journals people kept. There has been no more meticulous journal-keeper than the English preacher and reformer John Wesley. From him we can learn so much about life 200 years ago, including how they kept Ash Wednesday. In his journal for February 27, 1745, John Wesley records: "(Being Ash Wednesday.) After the public Prayers, the little church in our house met together. Misunderstandings were cleared up, and we all agreed to set out anew."[1] And later Wesley quotes the "Collect for Ash Wednesday" from the *Book of Common Prayer:* "Almighty God, who dost forgive the sins of them that are penitent, create and make in us new and contrite hearts; that we, worthily lamenting our sins, and acknowledging our wretchedness, may obtain of thee perfect remission and forgiveness, through Jesus Christ our Lord."[2]

A good beginning to our Lenten experience would be to pray that prayer with Wesley and all the saints who have gone before as well as with our fellow Christians today. And then we can go on to model our prayer life on Jesus' model prayer.

LORD, TEACH US TO PRAY

Have you ever felt like the disciples that day? As Luke tells it (11:1), Jesus was praying, undoubtedly in deep, close communication with His Father. And the disciples apparently waited—probably a little ways off, probably a little bemused by their Master's action (or lack of action), and probably not very patiently (especially if Peter was with them that day). At last "He ceased," and the disciples could ask Him about this. They knew prayer was important. They had seen its importance in Jesus' life, and they knew they didn't know enough about it. But they knew who to ask. And the world has benefited ever since from the answer they received.

We begin our journey into a deeper prayer life with the prayer our Lord gave to His disciples that day to teach us all how to pray. Studying and applying the principles in this prayer will form the basis of all our other praying. As Dallas Willard has said in his remarkable book *The Divine Conspiracy*, "The Lord's Prayer . . . is a foundation of the praying life: its introduction and its continuing basis. It is an enduring framework for all praying. You only move beyond it provided you stay within it. It is the necessary bass in the great symphony of prayer. It is a powerful lens through which one constantly sees the world as God himself sees it."[3]

In this light, it is appropriate that this is the prayer we will be studying through the Lenten season, because this is the season of petition and penance, from Ash Wednesday, on through the events upon which our whole Christian faith and our own salvation are based—the death and resurrection of our Lord Jesus Christ. Keep this fact central in your mind in the coming days, meditate on it to increase the power of this central fact in your own life.

As we think of our Lord's sacrifice and learn to model His prayer, we may be led to model His life in more active ways as well through the sacrificial acts of fasting and almsgiving that Christians have traditionally observed with special emphasis at this season. And we can draw closer in Christian community as we take part in special church services throughout the season, frequently repeating the Lord's Prayer together.

Beginning with the disciples gathered around Jesus requesting, "Lord, teach us to pray," this prayer has been central to Christians in both their private devotions and their corporate worship. The Lord's Prayer has been included as part of Communion services essentially from the beginning of the Church. In the sixth century the innovative Pope Gregory I directed that this prayer should be used as part of the consecration of the bread and the cup. Through its 2,000-year history the form of the prayer has altered only slightly—an amazing fact considering the changeableness of human beings.

In using the Lord's Prayer as a model, we need to consider the function accomplished by each phrase. First is the address or salutation—the "Our Father . . ."—which is similar to the greeting in a letter. I have a friend who is fond of reminding budding writers that no one sits down to write a letter—a nice, long, intimate letter—and then says, "Well, now—who shall I send this to?" In good letter-writing, like good conversation, we focus on the person to whom we are speaking. Likewise, in a prayer, we begin by focusing on the Person we are addressing. Active prayer is not a vague thought or feeling; it is not excitement or worrying. Real prayer is focused communication with a Person whom we are addressing personally.

Then follows the body of the prayer, the petitions. We are sometimes told, and in turn tell our children, that prayer is not a Christmas list. We shouldn't be forever asking for things when we pray, even if they are things for other people. But our Lord's teaching model does not bear out this idea. The very heart of His prayer is petition. The 18th-century divine Charles Simeon said, "Pleading with God is the very essence and perfection of prayer."[4] We are to ask God for our heart's deepest desires, trusting that these desires have been planted in our heart by Him. It is our job to request those things that will build the Kingdom.

The final part of the prayer is a great hymn of praise. This beautiful doxology can stand on its own as a prayer, or, combine the beginning and ending as a special prayer to the Father for His kingdom: "Our Father which art in heaven, Hallowed be thy name. Thy kingdom come. Thy will be done in earth, as it is in heaven. . . . For thine is the kingdom, and the power, and the glory, for ever. Amen."

We will be focusing on each section of the prayer as we walk through the steps of the Lord's Prayer in following His journey to the Cross in the coming weeks. In order to stay with the calendar, this "getting acquainted" chapter needs to be done the week before Lent begins. Week one should be done between Ash Wednesday and the first Sunday in Lent, that way Holy Week, which is really the sixth Sunday in Lent, can have its own special emphasis. In week 1 "Hallowed be thy name" leads us to focus on God's holiness, the lack of holiness in the world, and our need for personal holiness; in week 2 "In earth, as it is in heaven" explores the desire and possibility of experiencing heaven on earth; week 3 "Our daily bread" focuses our thoughts on trusting God for physical and spiritual needs, and we will see the connection between our regular meals and Holy Communion—we will even see that the Lord's Prayer is a summary of what takes place when we gather at the Lord's Table; in week 4, "Forgive us our debts," we look at our own need for confession, the place of confession in the life of the Church and the believing Christian, and our need to forgive others; in week 5 "Lead us" focuses on our need to seek and trust in God's guidance; and finally, in week 6, "The power, and the glory," we see the greatness of God and the place of praise and thanksgiving in prayer and worship.

That's a big chunk. We could easily do a whole book on this single prayer—many people have. And we could easily spend our whole lives praying this prayer. I trust that we will do exactly that.

Prayer Guide
Getting Acquainted with the Lord's Prayer

1. Prepare yourself and your environment for prayer and meditation. Make a physical place in your life for prayer. Choose a quiet spot. Keep your Bible, prayer journal, and devotional books nearby. Arrange a cross, candles, or religious pictures in your prayer corner. Choose a quiet time when children are in school or napping, when the telephone and other distractions can be turned off. Choose a comfortable chair or use a pillow to kneel on.

2. Pray the Lord's Prayer. Say each phrase aloud softly. After each phrase, pause and meditate on it. Add an emphasis in your own words. Record new insights you receive into this magnificent prayer and into your own spiritual needs.

3. Study your prayer list. Do the people, needs, situations on it fall into categories that fit under each petition? For example: Are you praying for specific world or local areas where you long to see God's will done as in heaven? Do you have material needs that fall into the "daily bread" category? Are others on your list struggling with hunger or other physical needs? Try arranging your prayer list in columns under each petition of the Lord's Prayer. (A word of advice: Experience has taught me to keep my prayer list in pencil, as I change it so frequently—especially to move requests to thanksgivings!)

C. S. Lewis calls this "festooning the Lord's Prayer." We are hanging our own petitions on the great petitions of Christ's model prayer just as we festoon a tree with garlands at Christmas—not to change the nature of the tree but to make it our own. We will continue to work with this process throughout Lent, so don't worry if you have empty areas on your list or things that don't quite make sense yet. If something fits perfectly, write it down. If not, wait for the Holy Spirit to guide you in your prayer life. After all, it's one of His special functions. "Likewise the Spirit also helpeth our infirmities: for we know not what we should pray for as we ought: but the Spirit itself maketh intercession for us with groanings which cannot be uttered" (Rom. 8:26).

Festooning the Lord's Prayer

"Hallowed be . . ."

Aspects of God's nature
I praise Him for

_____

_____

_____

_____

"Thy kingdom come"

World or local areas to
which God's kingdom
needs to come

_____

_____

_____

_____

"Thy will be done"

Situations in which God's
will needs to be done

_____

_____

_____

_____

"Our daily bread"

Material or spiritual
needs for myself or others

_____

_____

_____

_____

"Forgive us"

Things I need to be
forgiven for

_____

_____

_____

_____

"As we forgive"

People I need to forgive

_____

_____

_____

_____

"Lead us"

Things I'm seeking
God's guidance for

_____

_____

_____

_____

"Deliver us"

Areas where I or others
need special help

_____

_____

_____

_____

"The power and the glory"

Answers where God has
shown His power

_____

_____

_____

_____

2

The First Week in Lent: Preparation

Outside my window rain and mingled snow splash. Yet under the frowning, brown earth tender green shoots are beginning to stir. Soon windflowers and crocus will herald the coming green on trees, nesting birds, and golden daffodils. The glory of spring is coming, yet we must wait while the gray drizzle continues. Joy will come. But patience first.

Our study begins in the early spring season, the time of preparation for growth, the season the church calls Lent. Although the word *Lent* (from the Old Saxon word for spring) is not found in the Bible, our model for a season of preparation is Jesus, who went into the wilderness for 40 days of fasting before He began His ministry. Formal observance of Lent is a very ancient custom. In the second century Irenaeus, one of the earliest of the church fathers, speaks of it as an "old custom." In the year 325 Lent was established as part of the Church calendar by the Council of Nicaea. It seems to have been initiated for two purposes: To provide a period of regulated preparation for the adult converts to Christianity who were to be baptized at Easter (those coming into the church from the pagan world needed a lengthy time of teaching and preparing), and to set aside a time of extended fasting for established Christians to renew their spiritual lives. By the ninth century the number of adult converts had fallen off, so the season became more focused on penitence for believers.

Preparation is important for any event. Since Easter is the most important event in Christianity, it is vital that we prepare for it spiritually. As Robert Webber says, when we spend the six and a half weeks of Lent preparing our hearts for the risen Christ "Easter becomes a genuine personal experience of the resurrection."

Spend some time thinking about how you might prepare each area of your life: Time management—do you need to make more time for worship or for private devotions? Habits—do you need to adjust your leisure habits to make them more conducive to spiritual growth? Cooking or eating—are there changes you need to make so that your diet or your family's is healthier, physically or spiritually? Clothing and home accessories—would you or your family find it a helpful reminder of the season to add a touch of purple or violet to your surroundings?

Purple, the color for the Lenten season, is doubly appropriate as it's one of the traditional colors for mourning, as well as the color of royalty. Both sorrow for sin and awareness of Christ's royalty should be aspects of our observance of Lent.

"Hallowed be thy name"

A friend once remarked to me, "Americans have no understanding of the kingship of God because we have no national tradition of royalty." I have often thought about this as I see the supercasual way we live carry over in our often supercasual approach to the almighty God and Ruler of the universe. Likewise, we have very little concept of the holiness of God. As the world around us increasingly flaunts its profanity, the Church is affected, or infected, in subtle ways. In order to pray meaningfully we need to understand the nature of the God to whom we pray. He is "our Father," and we are privileged to approach Him boldly and to enjoy a close relationship with Him. But in enjoying this great privilege modern Americans are often in danger of overlooking the holiness and majesty of God.

We far prefer to focus on His mercy—that's more comfortable. "Oh, well, God is merciful. His grace will cover that." And we are very fortunate that, indeed, God is merciful, slow to anger, and full of grace. But it is one of those wonderful paradoxes of our faith that it is God's holiness that requires balance in His perfection of being. His mercy must be balanced by His justice.

Beginning our prayer by addressing our Father who is holy helps us focus all our thoughts on Him, raising our minds above the daily humdrum and entering into the highest heavenly courts. This entering into His presence should be a great help in overcoming the problem many people have of a wandering mind during prayer. If I were to enter the throne room at Buckingham Palace in the presence of Her Majesty Queen Elizabeth, I don't think I'd be having much trouble with my mind wandering off to what I was going to be doing later in the day. I think I'd be pretty focused on that moment. How much more so should we be when we enter the courts of heaven in prayer.

The holiness of God is clearly proclaimed throughout the Scriptures as one of the great themes of the Bible. In the Old Testament the holiness of God was reflected in everything connected with Him. The references abound to holy ground, holy convocation, holy Sabbath, holy nation, holy garments, holy things, holy gifts, holy oil, holy day, and on and on. But above all, His people were to be a holy people because the Holy One of Israel had called them to be so. The prophet Isaiah uses the phrase "Holy One of Israel" 34 times. God's holiness was to be feared, respected, worshiped, and reflected in His people. Lev. 11:44-45 says, "For I am the LORD your God: ye shall therefore sanctify yourselves, and ye shall be holy; for I am holy. . . . For I am the LORD that bringeth you up out of the land of Egypt, to be your God: ye shall therefore be holy, for I am holy."

And God's holiness was to inhabit the praises of His people. The psalmist says, "I will also praise thee with the psaltery, even thy truth, O my God: unto thee will I sing with the harp, O thou Holy One of Israel" (71:22); "Exalt ye the LORD our God, and worship at his footstool; for he is holy" (99:5); "Bless the LORD, O my soul: and all that is within me, bless his holy name" (103:1). I especially like Ps. 105:3 that says, "Glory ye in his holy name: let the heart of them rejoice that seek the LORD," because I feel that is exactly what we do when we pray "Hallowed be thy name." I don't know a better way to glory in His holy name.

The New Testament also proclaims God's holiness, but the emphasis is different. The theme of the New Testament is the work of the Holy Spirit in bringing the saving work of Christ to us. The great salvation story begins by telling how Mary was overcome by the Holy Ghost, Elizabeth was filled with the Holy Ghost, Zacharias was filled with the Holy Ghost, Joseph was assured by the Holy Ghost, Jesus was anointed with the Holy Ghost, the believers received the Holy Ghost. And Christ promised, "The Comforter, . . . the Holy Ghost, whom the Father will send in my name, . . . shall teach you all things, and bring all things to your remembrance, whatsoever I have said unto you" (John 14:26).

And because of God's holiness and the work of the Holy Spirit we can likewise be made holy by accepting Christ's sacrifice and presenting our "bodies a living sacrifice, holy, acceptable unto God" (Rom. 12:1). And in that way we can fulfill the commandment: "But as he which hath called you is holy, so be ye holy in all manner of conversation; because it is written, Be ye holy; for I am holy" (1 Pet. 1:15-16).

When we have thus had the image of a holy God restored in us, then even on earth we can truly join the heavenly throng that day and night praises God, saying, "Holy, holy, holy, Lord God Almighty, which was, and is, and is to come" (Rev. 4:8).

The Sanctus, which can be found in Christian worship services from as early as the second century, is one of the oldest prayers. It praises God's holiness and raises the worshiper to be with our Lord in the company of angels. This is the song sung by angels in Isaiah's vision of heaven, "Holy, holy, holy, is the LORD of hosts: the whole earth is full of his glory" (Isa. 6:3).

Throughout the nearly 2,000 years of Christian worship the Sanctus has taken different forms, some as elaborate as the settings given it by such composers as Bach, Beethoven, and Mozart, but the essence is contained in the simple words of the *Book of Common Prayer.* First is the prayer that ushers the worshipers into the presence of God: "Therefore with Angels and Archangels, and with all the company of heaven, we laud and magnify thy glorious Name; evermore praising thee, and saying."

Then the celebrant and people respond together: "Holy, holy, holy, Lord God of Hosts; Heaven and earth are full of thy glory. Glory be to thee, O Lord most High."

We could do much to restore our understanding of the One we are addressing in our prayers if we were to begin our own prayer by addressing God in these words.

Prayer Guide
Praying to a Holy God

1. Fix in your mind an image of God as the Holy One. Perhaps it will help to think of a stained-glass window or a great painting of Christ as King. Describe the image you see.

2. Look up scriptures that focus on God's holiness, such as 1 Sam. 2:2; 2 Chron. 16:10, 35; Ps. 99:9; Isa. 6:3; 57:15; Ezek. 39:7; Luke 1:49; Rev. 4:8; 15:4. Write your favorite verse in your journal.

3. Most hymnals have a section on God's holiness and majesty. Look up "Holy, Holy, Holy!" "Holy God, We Praise Thy Name," "Immortal, Invisible, God Only Wise," "Holiness unto the Lord," "Ye Servants of God," "The Lord Jehovah Reigns." Record some favorite lines.

4. Think about our world. Focus on the beauty and goodness that surround us. Then think of the ugliness and evil in the world. Even in the Church we often overlook the fact that we are worshiping a holy God. How might the Church change if we really saw God as holy?

How would our world be different if people in general regained a sense of the Holy?

What would I do differently if I truly hallowed His name?

5. Children reflect the image of their parents. As a child of a holy God, shouldn't my life reflect His holiness? Read Gen. 1:26a, 27. Write down your thoughts.

6. Write out what you really mean when you pray: "Our Father, which art in heaven, Hallowed be thy name."

7. Now go back to "Festooning the Lord's Prayer" on page 22 and consider your first list. Are there aspects of God's nature you need to add? Have you gained new understandings of qualities already on your list?

8. Pray the Lord's Prayer every day this week, pausing at the end of the salutation to repeat the Sanctus or your own praise to God's holiness.

3

The Second Week in Lent: Not Taking Away, Rather Adding To

My friend Betty asked me to teach her about observing Lent. Her questions were right to the point: "What should believers do during Lent? What should they not do?"

The first part is perhaps the easier. We should search our souls and our lives to learn how we can become more Christlike. This, of course, is something we should do all the time, but, especially in our frenzied world, it helps to have a specific time set aside on the calendar when the whole Christian community—in fellowship with those from earliest times—focuses on a similar journey.

What we should not do is more difficult, because it is more subtle and yet more concrete. My daughter's spiritual director is emphatic on the subject, "Lent isn't about giving something up. It's about adding something to your life."

The traditional idea of "I'm giving that up for Lent" can be a useful entry point, but it is not what the discipline is really about. If we choose to fast a food item, the money that would have been spent on chocolate, for example, might be given to the poor. Adding charity to our lives is the real point. The self-denial is a means to the end: it gives us more sympathy for those who might never be able to afford chocolate, and it makes funds available for us to donate.

Although abstinence from food or drink is the most usual form of fasting, any voluntary self-denial can be undertaken for the sake of spiritual growth. If we undertake to fast television watching, as my son did this year, the time saved can create an opportunity for more time spent in praying or meditating. If we choose to fast some type of popular reading, the time could be spent in Bible study. While in high school my daughter abstained from popular music on Sundays, even popular Christian music and listened only to hymns and classical music. Dan. 6:18 gives us a biblical example of fasting from music. And the apostle

Paul suggests another form of fasting—abstaining from the marital relationship for a time (1 Cor. 7:5) if both partners are in agreement.

A form of self-denial practiced through the ages, especially by those in religious orders, is fasting from talking. Refraining from casual chatter with those around us can create silent spaces where we can more clearly hear the voice of God. The beautiful novel *The Chosen* by Chaim Potok explores the powerful idea of raising a child with silence as a means of teaching him to encounter the Holy.

Whatever you choose to do about any specific discipline, keep in mind that Lent is a time to practice being with God, a time to set specific spiritual goals. Ask yourself, "Where do I want to be spiritually when I enter Holy Week this year?" Then undertake a discipline that will help you reach that goal, keeping in mind that Lent should be primarily a season of reflection and renewal. Taking up a discipline that leads to a frenzy of activity will be counterproductive.

And then, there are two other things I mentioned to Betty that we should not do: We should not be judgmental of those who spend the season serving the Lord in a different garden. The path outlined here is a path to a deeper spiritual life, but it isn't the only path. And we shouldn't fast on Sundays. Every Sunday is a "little Easter"—a commemoration of Jesus rising from the tomb—so it is a feast day. The Christian calendar takes this into account and the 40 days of Lent are calculated accordingly. Sundays are not included and therefore are referred to as "the First Sunday in Lent" not as "the First Sunday of Lent."

But lest we get bogged down in technicalities, let's turn to the words of the 17th-century poet Robert Herrick who reminds us how "To Keep a True Lent."

> *Is this a fast, to keep*
> *The larder lean,*
> *And clean*
> *From fat of veals and sheep?*
>
> *Is it to quit the dish*
> *Of flesh, yet still*
> *To fill*
> *The platter high with fish?*
>
> *Is it to fast an hour,*
> *Or ragg'd to go,*
> *Or show*
> *A downcast look, and sour?*
>
> *No; 'tis a fast, to dole*
> *Thy sheaf of wheat*
> *And meat*
> *Unto the hungry soul.*

It is to fast from strife,
From old debate,
And hate;
To circumcise thy life.

To show a heart grief-rent;
To starve thy sin,
Not thy bin;
And that's to keep thy Lent.

Remember, we're trying to learn how better to reflect the Christ who simply asked His followers to watch with Him for one hour. Can ye not do that?

"In earth, as it is in heaven"

"Thy kingdom come. Thy will be done in earth, as it is in heaven" is my favorite petition in the Lord's Prayer. I love to think of His kingdom truly coming to earth, of His will being done as completely here as it is done in heaven. This is the petition I spend the most time with in my own prayers. It really says it all, doesn't it? Wouldn't everything be taken care of if His will were done on earth as it is in heaven? Think of your own life—wouldn't everything be taken care of if His will controlled everything? Think of your family and friends, all those you pray for regularly. Is there anything you can ask for them more than that His will be done?

Think of our world—wouldn't all the problems be solved if His will were done here as in heaven? Well, yes—then it would be heaven, and we know that won't entirely happen here because we live in a fallen world. And yet, Christ taught us to pray for that very thing—so there is hope! The more we pray for this, the closer our world can come to His will being done completely. Pray it for yourself, for your family, for revival for our nation, for revival in any world area you are particularly concerned about. Let praying this petition help you develop the desire and realize the possibility of experiencing heaven on earth.

At first glance "Thy kingdom come. Thy will be done . . ." looks like two petitions. This, however, is really a very good example of the typical characteristic of Hebrew literary style, which we encounter so often in the Psalms—that of parallelism—saying something a second time in different words for the sake of emphasis. When His kingdom is fully come to earth, His will shall be fully done here.

And the only place to start is in my own heart. "Father, let Your kingdom come to my heart. Let Your will be done as fully in my heart and in my life as it is done in heaven." This is the foundation and sum total of the Christian life—doing God's will fully. And desiring to see it done in all the world.

So we must start by applying this petition inward, to our own hearts, then we can apply it outward, to the rest of our world: Thy kingdom come to my home and family, thy kingdom come to my neighborhood and church, thy kingdom come to my nation, thy kingdom come to the whole world. Let thy will be done in all the earth as completely as it is done in heaven. And because prayer is always circular, we again look into our own hearts for the specific people and places God has given us a burden to pray for. What family members or friends do you most long to see come into or growing in the Kingdom? Where in the world do you most long to see God's grace outpoured in revival and spiritual renewal? Insert the names of those people and places when you pray this petition.

John Wesley formed a complete prayer of this petition: "May Thy kingdom of grace come quickly, and swallow up all the kingdoms of the earth! May all mankind, receiving Thee, O Christ, for their King, truly believing in Thy name, be filled with righteousness and peace and joy, with holiness and happiness, till they are removed hence into Thy kingdom of glory to reign with thee for ever and ever."[1]

Because the Lord's Prayer was given to the Church by the Lord himself, it has always been regarded as uniquely sacred and used in that most sacred of Christian events, the celebration of the Lord's Supper. It is often prayed in conjunction with that part of the service called the Epiclesis where the presence of the Holy Spirit is invoked at the Communion table. This is particularly appropriate when we consider the fact that some early manuscripts replaced "thy kingdom come" with "may thy Holy Spirit come upon us and cleanse us."

And the Lord's Prayer has always played a central role in the private devotions of Christian giants through the ages as well. Tertullian, one of the earliest of the church fathers, called it "the epitome of the whole Gospel," Augustine called it the "source of all other prayers," and the 16th-century mystic Teresa of Avila said this prayer contained in it "the entire spiritual way."

In her private prayers Teresa used the opening words of the prayer to lead into her own extemporaneous prayer, but always returned to our Lord's words as the central ground of her prayer life. She believed that the Lord gave us this prayer in unspecific terms so that each one could petition according to his or her own intention. She liked to pray, "Your kingdom come within us," because "He provided for us by giving us here on earth His kingdom."

For "Thy will be done in earth, as it is in heaven," Teresa said, "Certainly, Lord, if You hadn't made the petition, the task would seem to me impossible. But when Your Father does what You ask Him . . . the possibility is there for Your will to be done in me." These are words I can take comfort in whether I am applying this petition to my desire for God's will to be done in my own life or my desire to see revival in a distant land.

Prayer Guide
Praying for Heaven on Earth

1. The beauty of God the Creator is reflected in the beauty of His creation.

Spend some time in quiet contemplation of the beauty of the earth. List some of your favorite images.

2. Now think of places where the image of the Creator has been defaced by evil. How would these places, situations, people be different if God's kingdom came to them?

3. Look up the following scriptures and record what you learn about the will of God: Rom. 12:2; 2 Cor. 8:5; Gal. 1:4; Eph. 6:6; Col. 4:12; 1 Thess. 4:3-7; 5:18-25; Heb. 10:36; 1 Pet. 1:15; 4:2, 19; 1 John 2:17.

4. What is your greatest struggle in doing God's will in your own life?

Have you undertaken a Lenten discipline and set a goal for spiritual growth to help you see God's will done in this?

5. List in your journal the spiritual needs of people dear to you for whom God's will needs to be done.

6. List your prayer burden for missionaries or for world areas in need of spiritual renewal.

7. Turn back to page 22. Do you need to add new items under "Thy kingdom come" or "Thy will be done"? Have you seen answers to prayer in these areas since you began the list? If so, write those items under "The power and the glory."

4 The Third Week in Lent: Dinner's Ready!

Have you ever stopped to think how many times you've said that in your life? Or if you're not the cook where you live, how many times you've waited to hear it? My husband and I have been married for 35 years. I'm the cook (we're very traditional). That means I must have said, "Dinner's ready!" something like 12,775 times. And that doesn't begin to calculate how many times I've answered the question, "What's for dinner?" I used to long for the luxury of being able to ask someone that question myself. Then I discovered how to do it: Put casseroles in the freezer without marking them—then I wouldn't know what it was either.

But seriously, have you thought of the times when Jesus said essentially that? At the feeding of the 5,000, when He cooked fish on the seashore after the Resurrection, when He instituted the Lord's Supper. Throughout the Bible, in the festivals of the children of Israel and the gatherings of the New Testament Church, and on throughout the history of the Church beginning right from the first century as Christians gathered to reenact the story of their salvation, food has played a central role.

I recently attended a Communion service being celebrated by a woman minister. At that beautiful moment in the service where she held up the elements and said, "The gifts of God for the people of God. Take them in remembrance that Christ died for you, and feed on Him in your hearts by faith, with thanksgiving," I thought, "That's just like a mother telling her family to come to dinner."

It's no wonder, then, that food plays a central role in the matter of Lenten disciplines for those seeking a deeper spiritual life. We've already discussed the matter of fasting. In this lesson we need to look more closely at the other traditional Lenten discipline, almsgiving. One of my favorite historical persons and a model of one who lived a charitable life is Margaret, the 11th-century Queen of Scots. Margaret of Scotland was one of the most beloved and highly honored queens of all time. Margaret loved God and loved her people. She set about teaching her people to love God by showing them God's love, especially in feeding and caring for the poor.

It was said of Margaret of Scotland that "she was poorer herself than all her poor: for they had not, but desired to have; while she took pains to scatter what she had."[1] It could almost become comical at times because when she went about the countryside she would give everything she had with her to the poor; then, when she had given her all she would begin commanding her attendants and courtiers to give their jewels and cloaks to the needy. Not even King Malcolm was allowed to escape Margaret's charitable impulses when she saw a beggar without a coat.

And Margaret delighted in saying, "Dinner's Ready!" to her beloved poor. It was her custom to feed 300 poor on Maundy Thursday—she and Malcolm serving them with their own hands in the royal hall. She also fed nine baby orphans, taking them on her lap and spoon-feeding soft foods she had ordered especially. In addition, 24 poor people were fed year-round in the royal hall. By her own example Margaret changed a nation, teaching them to follow Christ's command to "Feed my lambs."

Another person who set a high standard of charity and changed his world was John Wesley. In January of 1740 he recorded in his journal, "I made a collection in our congregation for the relief of the poor, who having no work, (because of the severe frost,) and no assistance from the parish wherein they lived, were reduced to the last extremity. I made another collection on Thursday; and a third on Sunday; by which we were enabled to feed a hundred, sometimes a hundred and fifty, a day, of those whom we found to need it most."[2]

And in May of 1741 he said that he reminded the society that many among them were without food and clothing. "I had done what in me lay to feed the hungry, to clothe the naked, to employ the poor, and to visit the sick; but was not, alone, sufficient for these things; and therefore desired all whose hearts were as my heart, 1. To bring what clothes each could spare, to be distributed among those that wanted most. 2. To give weekly a penny, or what they could afford, for the relief of the poor and sick."[3]

Wesley suggested that, "if every Christian family, while in health, would thus far deny themselves, would twice a week dine on the cheapest food, drink in general herb-tea, faithfully calculate the money saved thereby, and give it to the poor over and above their usual donations, we should then hear no complaining in our streets, but the poor would eat and be satisfied."[4]

Wesley's summary of true Christian economy can be summed up in his sermon titled "The Use of Money": "Gain all you can, without hurting either yourself or your neighbour . . . ; save all you can, by cutting off every expense which serves only to indulge foolish desire . . . ; and then, give all you can, or, in other words, give all you have to God . . . that whatever ye do may be 'a sacrifice of a sweet-smelling savour to God.'"[5]

We can all think of many other people we know or have read of, such as Mother Teresa, who have changed their world by applying the rule: "If there be among you a poor man . . . thou shalt not harden thine heart, nor shut thine hand from thy poor brother: but thou shalt open thine hand wide unto him" (Deut. 15:7-8). Not many of us can be Queen Margarets, John Wesleys, or Mother Teresas, but we can all do something to feed the lambs around us, and there is no better time to make a special effort in this direction than during Lent.

"Give us this day our daily bread"

One of my favorite things about praying this petition is that it helps me see the connection between our regular meals and the Lord's Supper. As a wife and mother who has to produce three meals a day every day of my life, it's important to see a spiritual dimension to my most mundane tasks, and just as a priest's highest calling is to prepare and serve the Communion elements, so my highest calling is in serving my family. And this vision helps me try to make every family gathering around the table a time of real communion where we fellowship with each other and remember that God is with us. Such a vision can transform your family life.

William Barclay recounts that for centuries there was much scholarly disagreement over the meaning of this petition because the Greek word translated "daily" was unknown in any other ancient manuscript. As a matter of fact, it was believed that Matthew invented the Greek word he had used *(epiousios)* until a papyrus fragment was found with the word on it. And the fragment was a woman's shopping list! She was reminding herself to buy a certain food for her family for the coming day.

How well I can relate to that wife and mother in ancient Greece. How many times I've entered the crowded grocery store tired and hurried, looked at my often indecipherable shopping list and prayed, "Lord, help me to get what my family needs." And, always, He gives us our daily bread, just as faithfully as He provided manna for the children of Israel in the wilderness.

"Give us this day our daily bread" encompasses all our needs—physical, material, and spiritual—and praying this helps us trust God for their fulfillment. The very fact that He invites us to pray for these needs means He is longing to meet them. Think of that—isn't that exciting! The great God of the universe, Creator and Sustainer of all, wants to fill my needs, is waiting for me to ask!

Likewise, we can pray this petition for the poor, the hungry, the victims of disaster around the world. If anyone has trouble rounding out his or her prayer list for this petition, he or she need only glance at the daily newspaper to find abundant examples of people in need of their daily bread. And, of course, although we can take the petition literally as applying to our need for food, it applies to all our physical needs as well. How many mornings I look at my schedule and pray for strength for the day. And Christ, the Bread of Heaven, gives His strength. When friends tell me of needs for their families or their employment problems, or I read of missionaries in need, I add their names to this petition.

The literal, physical application of this petition is important. God cares about our physical bodies, and food is our most basic need. But most important of all is the spiritual application of this petition. Our daily bread is our daily communion with the One who said, "I am the living bread which came down from heaven: if any man eat of this bread, he shall live for ever: and the bread that I will give is my flesh, which I will give for the life of the world" (John 6:51). And just as the children of Israel in the wilderness couldn't store up manna, but had to rely on the daily renewal of God's supply, so we need to seek our spiritual food daily.

Perhaps the best summary of the meaning of this petition is John Wesley's from his *Explanatory Notes upon the New Testament:* "Give us, O Father (for we claim nothing of right, but only Thy free mercy), this day (for we take no thought for the morrow) our daily bread—All things needful for our souls and bodies; not only 'the meat that perisheth,' but the sacramental bread, and Thy grace, the food 'which endureth to everlasting life.'"[6] Amen.

Prayer Guide
Praying for our Daily Bread

1. Recall a special charitable act that you have been privileged to perform or one you have read of another doing. Record it in your journal.

2. Read Deut. 15:7-8 and Isa. 58:5-10. What do these passages say to you about charity? Write out your answers.

3. Recall a time when you or your family have been in special need physically or spiritually.

How was this need met?

4. What specific needs do you or your family face this day? List them in your journal.

5. Are you praying for others with needs for physical or spiritual bread?

6. Read carefully John 6:5-58. What lessons do you see here?

How can you apply Christ's words to your life? Do you need to rely more on Christ to meet your needs? Do you need to give more of Him to others? Do you need to spend more time in His Word? Do you need to take Communion more often?

7. Look up the old gospel song, "Come and Dine." It contains references to six scriptural instances of God supplying our daily bread. List them in your journal.

8. Look back at your answers to questions 4 and 5, then turn back to page 22 and festoon "our daily bread" with names and needs.

5

The Fourth Week in Lent: Faults! Who? Me?

The crush of fashionable coaches outside number 14 Park Lane facing Hyde Park was not an unusual sight in mid-18th-century London. It meant that the Countess of Huntingdon had issued another of her summons to her aristocratic friends that they were to come to her drawing room to hear one of her favorite preachers. Today it was to be George Whitefield, newly returned from a preaching mission to the American colonies.

As the Dowager Duchess of Buckingham reached the top of the pillared portico she flipped her lace fan and swished her fashionably wide petticoats. It was obvious she saw little to be gained from an afternoon spent singing the songs of Mr. Charles Wesley and listening to the enthusiasms of any preacher—even one so glowingly endorsed by Lady Huntingdon.

Whitefield preached one of his most stirring sermons on the necessity of confession and forgiveness, abetted by crashing thunder and streaking lightning outside the windows. But the duchess in her silver-embroidered, ribbed silk gown was unmoved. "I thank your Ladyship for the information," she took leave of her hostess. "But I find his doctrine repulsive. It is strongly tinctured with impertinence and disrespect toward his superiors."

She turned toward all the room and tapped her walking stick on the parquet floor. "It is monstrous to be told that you have a heart as sinful as the common wretches that crawl upon the earth. I find this highly offensive and insulting." With a toss of her head, she left.

Not many of us would react so dramatically as the Dowager Duchess of Buckingham when told that sinners need to repent, and yet how many Christians recoil inside with considerable vehemence to a suggestion that we need to confess? "I'm a Christian, Christ has forgiven my sins. What do I have to confess?" And yet, that's exactly what our Lord told us to do in His model prayer: "Forgive us our trespasses."

We are now halfway through Lent, and if you've been trying to follow a new Lenten discipline such as fasting or almsgiving, perhaps you will see some need for confession as you look back over the past weeks. Remember, one of the meanings of *trespasses* is "shortcomings."

I always find myself with plenty of shortcomings for which I need forgiveness. Even if I haven't broken my fast, my attitudes have often been less than perfect. Even if I've made progress toward my goal of new spiritual growth, I have not reached as far as I'd hoped. Even if I've done some extra act of charity, there's so much I've left undone.

And that's what this midpoint of Lent is all about. Laetare Sunday, or Refreshment Sunday, is the name given to the fourth Sunday in Lent. Rose, the color of joy, is the liturgical color for the day, and in many churches Isa. 66:10 is read, "Rejoice ye with Jerusalem, and be glad with her . . . rejoice with joy for her." In England this day is known as Mothering Sunday, where it is traditional to visit one's mother and also to attend "mother church." The traditional food is simnel cake, a wonderfully rich fruitcake with inches of marzipan filling—the eating of which signals a relaxation of Lenten fasting for the day.

But in more practical terms (although I would defend simnel cake as a thoroughly practical idea) the point of Refreshment Sunday is to relax and take stock of one's Lenten progress. Confess any shortcomings, reset your vision on your goals, and carry on. And so it's most appropriate that this week we will learn to pray "forgive us our trespasses" in a new way.

"Forgive us . . ."

The petition "forgive us our trespasses, as we forgive those who trespass against us" forces us to examine our own lives with a fine-toothed comb. Whether you belong to the branch of the Church that believes we sin daily in word, thought, and deed; or are among those that hold the theological understanding that through the power of the Holy Spirit it is possible to live above willful sin; whether you attend a church that regularly incorporates a general confession into their worship service; or you believe that confession of sins is done once and for all, we have here our Lord's model that we are to examine our lives carefully and regularly to ask for forgiveness for any shortcoming the Holy Spirit shows us.

William Barclay says that before a person can honestly pray this petition he or she must realize the need to pray it. That is, there must be a sense of sin. And sin is no more popular today than it was in the Duchess of Buckingham's day—or perhaps I should say, sin is just as popular as it was then—it's confessing that's unpopular. But for most of us the real problem is understanding what sin really is. We would have no problem understanding that we needed to confess and ask forgiveness for the sins of murder, stealing, lying, or adultery. But what about the sin of imperfection? Oops.

I very much like the "Confession of Need" quoted in the *Wollaston Service Book:* "O God, you have shown us the way of life through your Son, Jesus Christ. We confess with shame our slowness to learn of him, our failure to follow him, and our reluctance to bear the cross. We confess the poverty of our worship, our neglect of fellowship and of the means of grace, our hesitating witness for Christ, our evasion of responsibility in our service, and our imperfect stewardship of your gifts." It expresses so much of what I need to confess.

Our "Festooning the Lord's Prayer" chart can be an enormous help in getting this concept of confession into perspective. The first time I tried filling in the "Things I need to be forgiven for" column my list was pretty sketchy. Let's face it—I'm not perfect, but I try. After all, I'm not living in rebellion to any known law of God. But the deeper I got into understanding and praying the Lord's Prayer, the more harshly the mirror of His nature showed up my own flaws.

Look at your first column where you've listed aspects of God's nature for which you praise Him. Among attributes I have listed there are: holiness, grace, creativity, beauty, patience, faithfulness. As His children we are to reflect Him in all things. All things? Even holiness and patience and . . . ? Oh, my. If sin is to be rightly understood as a falling short of His perfection, how very, very much I have to confess and beg forgiveness for!

". . . as we forgive"

And then you'll notice something different here—this petition has an add-on. This reminds me of the commandment to "honour thy father and thy mother," which is the only commandment with an add-on—"that thy days may be long upon the land." The add-on to asking for forgiveness for our transgressions is that we forgive those who transgress against us. Oops—"But wait a minute, Lord. Did You hear what she said to me?" "Well, but that person was really rotten to me." "Sure, I'd be perfectly willing to forgive him if he asked—but he hasn't." Umm—that isn't what it says, is it? "Forgive us—as we forgive." In his famous sermon "The Weight of Glory" C. S. Lewis said, "To be a Christian means to forgive the inexcusable, because God has forgiven the inexcusable in you."

Now perhaps a name, or even several names, springs forcefully to your mind whenever you pray "as we forgive those who trespass against us." If so, you haven't had much trouble filling out that column on your chart. At least, I hope you haven't had trouble, because simply admitting the need to forgive is that all-important first step. And if you haven't been able to pray the forgiving bit with conviction because you haven't been able actually to forgive, simply ask God to do it for you. Being willing to be willing is the key.

But what if you're one of the lucky ones? Most people have treated you rather decently as you've gone through life, and those that haven't you've been able to overlook. You just naturally don't carry grudges. Some people are like that. They probably just naturally have low blood pressure too. It's nice, but not necessarily a virtue—it's just the way they're made. So what do you do about festooning that petition if you're one of those people? Try praying, "As I forgive those who disagree with me." Now there's something that makes me see red. Rudeness I can forgive. (It's not their fault if their mother didn't teach them manners, I tell myself.) Ill intent I can forgive. (We know we live in a fallen world and all will be made right in the next.) But wrongheadedness and stupidity drive me up the wall. Now there's something I need to pray about, something I need to be forgiven for.

"To be unforgiven," my pastor said, "is to walk around bearing all the weight and burden of our transgressions, while all the power of forgiveness is waiting there for us if we so choose." Through accepting our Lord's forgiveness all the energy we waste dealing with hurts and insults can be poured into working for good.

Charles Simeon, the 18th-century English preacher and scholar, says that the forgiveness we exercise toward others is not to be understood as the measure of that which we receive from God, because everything we do is so extremely imperfect, but God's mercy to us should be the pattern with which we treat our offending fellow creatures: That is, by forgiving freely, fully, cordially, and forever.

Our Lord tells us that if we come to the altar "and there rememberest that thy brother hath aught against thee; leave there thy gift before the altar, and go thy way; first be reconciled to thy brother, and then come and offer thy gift" (Matt. 5:23-24). We are to make things right with our brothers and our sisters before we bring our gifts to the altar.

The Reverend Richard Demerest said in a recent sermon, "Christ's wounds are the proof of the abundance of His forgiveness. His wounds —and the fact that He lives. So we can choose to avail ourselves of His power. His breath—the same breath that breathed life into creation is there to breathe on us with its power to create us anew if we will permit it. The power of the resurrection gives us the power—the ability—to forgive. In the resurrection God established the covenant of reconciliation."

It is through praying this petition for forgiveness and forgiving others that we accept Christ's invitation to, "Come unto me, all ye that labour and are heavy laden, and I will give you rest" (Matt. 11:28).

Prayer Guide
Praying for Forgiveness and Forgiving

1. At this midpoint in Lent, pause to consider where you are in your Lenten journey. Have you undertaken a spiritual discipline? Have you set spiritual goals? What progress have you made?

What problems have you encountered?

Have you asked forgiveness for failures? What new intentions have you undertaken? Write them down.

2. How do you feel about the idea of confessing: In private prayer? To another person?

As an act of corporate worship?

3. Turn to your festooning chart on page 22. Study your list of qualities of God for which you praise Him. Does this bring to mind shortcomings in your own life for which you need to ask forgiveness? If so, write them in your "Forgive us" column.

4. Are there people you need to forgive: People in your life now who have hurt, angered, or mistreated you? (Remember this can range from actual abuse to simple irritation.) People who live at a distance or don't even know you personally (such as political or religious leaders) but whose actions have offended you? People from the past, perhaps long dead, from your own family or from history, the result of whose actions you must still cope with? Put their names (or their actions if you don't know their names) under "People I Need to Forgive."

5. Note that list is for people I need to forgive, not "people I have forgiven." What problems do you face in forgiving?

If you are unable to forgive, are you willing to have God make you willing?

6. If you need to forgive someone in your past, one of the most powerful methods is to write a letter to that person. If the letter is undeliverable, you might want simply to keep it or perhaps burn it with a prayer. If the person is dead, visit their grave if possible. Read the letter to them, talk to them, or pray with them.

7. Read Matt. 5:22-24. How can you apply this to your own life?

8. Look up these comfortable words of forgiveness: Matt. 11:28; John 3:16; 1 Tim. 1:15; 1 John 2:1-2. What comfort did you receive? Write about the experience in your journal.

6 The Fifth Week in Lent: Red Light/Green Light

Almighty God, you alone can bring into order the unruly wills and affections of sinners: Grant your people grace to love what you command and desire what you promise; that, among the swift and varied changes of the world, our hearts may surely there be fixed where true joys are to be found; through Jesus Christ our Lord, who lives and reigns with you and the Holy Spirit, one God, now and forever. Amen." As we seek God's leading in our lives this week we can do no better than to begin with this prayer for the Fifth Sunday in Lent from the *Book of Common Prayer.*

With only two weeks left in Lent it's appropriate that we focus on the role of our Lord to guide and protect us. May the Father, God of Abraham, Isaac, and Moses who led the children of Israel with a pillar of smoke by day and a pillar of fire by night; the Son, the Good Shepherd who leads us beside still waters; and the Spirit, the Comforter who is come to lead us into all truth, guide us in this lesson and in our prayer time this week that we will walk ever closer in His Truth, Goodness, and Beauty.

This week I am drawn to look back at the first Sunday in Lent when the lessons in many churches laid out the whole history of temptation in the world, beginning with the story of Adam and Eve in the garden (Gen. 2:4—3:24), Christ being led of the Spirit into the wilderness to be tempted of the devil (Matt. 4:1-11); with the two stories culminating in the assurance that "as by the offence of one [Adam's sin] judgment came upon all men to condemnation; even so by the righteousness of one [Christ's righteousness] the free gift came upon all men unto justification of life" (Rom. 5:18).

From this we can see that, even if the self-examination and penitence of Lent are seeming to drag on, we can look ahead to the triumphal end of the story. It seems that much of what we learn from following the Church calendar is the discipline of waiting; as a matter of fact, I think it's much of what I've learned from life—or am trying to learn. So no matter how tempted we may be to leap ahead to the end of the story and sing "Up from the grave He arose, / With a mighty triumph o'er His foes," we're still in Lent and still must sing: "Lord, who throughout these forty days for us didst fast and pray, teach us with thee to mourn our sins, and close by thee to stay. As thou with Satan didst contend and didst the victory win, O give us strength in thee to fight, in thee to conquer sin. As thou didst hunger bear and thirst, so teach us, gracious Lord, to die to self, and chiefly live by thy most holy word. And through these days of penitence, and through thy Passiontide, yea, evermore, in life and death, Jesus with us abide" (Claudia Frances Hernaman).

"Lead us not into temptation"

The Cambridge undergraduate drug his feet as he made his way along the yellow gravel path in front of King's College Chapel to the Gibbs Building. The Hon. Granville Ryder looked over his shoulder at a lively group headed for a party in a friend's room. They were a jolly fine bunch of fellows. Besides, he had rather serious misgivings about attending one of Charles Simeon's little conversation parties. No matter how much a feature of Cambridge life these gatherings had become. And no matter how illustriously evangelical Granville's family was— even if he didn't live up to it.

Taking a determined grip on the edges of his black academic robe, Granville climbed the four flights of dark, narrow stairs, entered the spacious room filled with rows of benches, most of them occupied by gownsmen, and accepted a cup of tea, wishing it were something stronger. Simeon had begun these little parties in his rooms some 20 years earlier as a means of giving the undergraduates, most of whom were to take holy orders in the Church of England, at least some smattering of religious instruction. It was Simeon's rather eccentric belief that young men needed something more than an education in mathematics and the classics to prepare them for the ministry.

And so they gathered weekly to ask questions of the vicar of Holy Trinity Church whose *Expository Outlines on the Whole Bible* would someday be a classic. When 60 or 70 gownsmen had squeezed into the room, Simeon took his accustomed elevated seat by the fireplace, folded his hands upon his knees, and said, "Now, if you have any questions to ask, I shall be happy to hear them, and to give what assistance I can."

Immediately the room was alive with the questions of young ordinands. The discussion soared to theological realms beyond Granville's grasp or interest. He looked around, contemplating pushing a path to the door and joining his friends at cards. But before he could make a move a thin young man right behind him asked Simeon about the temptation of repentant Christians. Simeon nodded. "Ah, indeed, and so wisely did our Lord teach us to pray, 'lead us not into temptation,' for temptations present themselves to us on every side. Every thing that is agreeable to our senses or flattering to our minds, has a tendency to draw us from God. Even the things which are the most innocent when moderately enjoyed, often become snares to us. Our food, our raiment, our comforts of every kind, and even our dearest relatives, are apt to en-

gross our affections too much, and to become the objects of an idola-
trous regard—the cares and troubles of life also are frequently sources
of unbelieving anxiety, or murmuring discontent."

Granville, who knew well the pull of all such temptations, settled
back on his seat, not sure whether to find encouragement in the fact
that the learned man so well understood the situation, or to be even
more discouraged by the acknowledged power of evil. "So how are we
then to be kept from such power?" a voice from the far side of the room
spoke Granville's thoughts.

"Therefore must we pray to be kept from the power of temptations."
Simeon punctuated his statement with a rapid, forceful gesture that
emphasized his words. "God will often put an obstacle in the way of his
people, so as to keep them from executing the evil suggestions of their
hearts: He will plant a 'hedge.' This he can do in ten thousand ways,
without at all infringing upon the liberty of the human will.

"Moreover, he has promised to do this in answer to our prayers. He
will either make a way for us to escape from the temptations that as-
sault us; or will moderate them, so that they may not be too powerful
for us; or increase our strength, that we may be able to overcome them.
In a word, he will 'order our goings' and 'direct our paths.' If we were to
depend on our own wisdom, we should only increase the difficulties
which we designed to avoid; but if we make God our refuge, we shall be
preserved. He has bidden us 'watch and pray that we enter not into
temptation;' and he will never suffer us to use these means in vain."

It all sounded so simple. Granville looked at his fellow undergraduates filling the room. They looked so intent, so calm. Could any of them
have struggles like his? Could any have fallen as many times as he had
fallen? Could he come through his struggles to find such a security as
they seemed to have? "Can we hope to be kept from every temptation?"
The words were out before Granville realized he had spoken.

"But, my dear fellow, of course we can't!" Simeon's sharp-featured
face broke into a broad smile as if he were delivering good news rather
than a pronouncement of doom. "You see, we have two foes: our own
in-dwelling corruptions which would yield to temptation; and the outward enemy—Satan, a great and powerful enemy. The words of our
Lord's prayer which are translated 'deliver us from evil' might better be
rendered 'deliver us from the evil one.' Satan is represented in Scripture
as a most subtle and cruel adversary to man. He is called a serpent for
his subtlety, a dragon for his fierceness, and a god for the dominion that
he exercises over the children of men. To withstand him in our own
strength is impossible.

"Therefore are we instructed to pray to be delivered from him. God
will deliver us from the tempter as well as from temptation. He has provided armour for us, which, if used aright, shall defend us against all his
fiery darts. Does any one ask, How shall I get this armour? We answer,

Pray to God to give it you. It is by prayer that it is obtained; by prayer it is put on; by prayer we are rendered expert in the use of it; and by prayer our heart is steeled with courage, and our arm confirmed with strength. The petition the Lord taught us in His model prayer will answer every end; and urged with frequency and faith, will soon make us more than conquerors."

The image of the bold warrior gleamed in Granville's mind but was quickly replaced by the picture of the many times he had attempted to stride forward, always to be knocked down lower than he had been before.

Simeon's next words were as if he, too, had seen such an image. "And so shall 'God's strength be perfected in our weakness,' if only we rely on him for our deliverance: were we a thousand times weaker than we are, his grace should assuredly be sufficient for us. No matter how painful your trial may be, remember, that Satan is a vanquished enemy. He cannot go beyond the limits which God has assigned him, and your God is ever at hand to hear and answer your petitions. Were you called to contend in your own strength, your situation would be tremendous; but you are commanded to 'cast your care on God, who careth for you,' and to 'encourage yourselves in the Lord your God.' Be strong then, and fear not: 'be strong in the Lord and in the power of his might': and know that he who has taught you to look to him for guidance and protection, will 'keep you from falling.'"

As Granville bowed his head he felt a tightness, an anxiety, that had long held him at the breaking point relax within him.

Perhaps some of us today, like Granville Ryder almost 200 years ago, have struggled and failed often in the face of temptation. Our Lord, who "was in all points tempted like as we are" (Heb. 4:15), knew all about that when He gave us this most comforting of the petitions—"Lead us not into temptation [or as the original Greek says, 'into trying circumstances'], but deliver us from evil."

Think a moment. What images does that phrase conjure in your mind? Do you think of the Good Shepherd and the 23rd psalm—green pastures and still waters? Or of Isa. 40:11, "He shall feed his flock like a shepherd: he shall gather the lambs with his arm, and carry them in his bosom, and shall gently lead those that are with young"? Or how about God leading the children of Israel with a pillar of fire by day and a pillar of smoke by night? And sometimes I like to go farther afield and recall the wonderful images of God's leading and deliverance portrayed in Bunyan's *Pilgrim's Progress*. But whatever vision comes to your mind, there could not possibly be anything more comforting than the knowledge that God himself offers to lead us through this life—to keep us safe from temptation and evil and to bring us triumphantly into His kingdom!

Prayer Guide
Praying for Guidance

1. Last week we looked at the first step in the Christian life—asking forgiveness for our sins. This week's petition leads us on into the deeper life. Charles Simeon says, "The obtaining of pardon would satisfy a person who was merely alarmed by the terrors of hell: but a truly regenerate person will desire deliverance from sin as much as from hell itself. Hence, having implored pardon for his past sins, he will, with equal earnestness, desire victory over his remaining corruptions. But how is this victory to be gained, seeing that we are encompassed with temptations, and assaulted by all the powers of darkness? It must be gained by committing ourselves to the care of our heavenly Father, and by seeking from Him the guidance of His providence."[1] Have you made this deeper, total commitment of your life, not merely to turn from sin, but also to seek His will in all things?

2. In lesson 3 we prayed that God's will would be done on earth as it is in heaven. This is how that prayer can be made a reality in our own lives and our own bit of the earth—by asking Him to lead in all things and by submitting fully to His guidance. God guides in many ways, some quiet and some dramatic. Look up two hymns that exemplify very different aspects of God's guidance. "Savior, like a Shepherd Lead Us" is a beautiful, calm picture of God leading His sheep with tender care in pleasant pastures. "Lead On, O King Eternal" is a picture of a militant, conquering God leading His people forth into battle. Describe in your journal times when you have known each type of leading.

3. We cannot avoid "trying circumstances" or being defeated by temptations without God's guidance. What are some trying circumstances you fear or temptations you struggle with?

4. In "The Man Who Corrupted Hadleyburg," a story by Mark Twain, a sign posted outside a town read, "Lead us not into temptation." The people were smug and happy until one day a stranger came into town with a mysterious bag of gold. Because the town had known no temptation and had no experience resisting, they were torn apart. At the end they changed their motto to "Lead us into temptation." Since we know we can grow from struggles and be strengthened by overcoming temptation through God's power, how can it be right to pray "lead us not into temptation"? How can facing temptations strengthen us?

5. Praying for God's guidance ("lead us") is a prayer that looks ahead. What are the circumstances ahead in your life for which you especially need God's leading?

Are there special places or activities you hope God will lead you into?

What areas of God's leadership are you praying for family or friends?

6. Praying for deliverance ("deliver us from evil") looks at the past. Are there things in your past you need deliverance from?

What areas do you know of where others need special help?

7. Add items from questions 5 and 6 to your festooned Lord's Prayer on page 22.

7

The Sixth Week
in Lent:
Coming Full Circle

An English teacher once told me, and as an English teacher I have often told students, "A unified piece of writing 'hangs together' much like a sculpture. When your writing coheres, all parts relate in such a way they form a continuous whole—including the beginning and the end.

"Recurrence is the easiest way to experience coming full circle; it is a repetition in your ending of some aspect of your beginning. The strongest image of 'full-circle wholeness' is the picture of a snake biting its own tail."[1]

Here we are at the end of Lent and at the end of the Lord's Prayer, and for both the image of the snake biting his tail is appropriate. Look back at chapter 1 where we first discussed the idea of undertaking a special spiritual discipline for Lent. Review chapter 3 where we talked about considering where you wanted to be spiritually when you entered Holy Week and setting a spiritual goal for the Lenten season. Did you set a goal? Have you made spiritual progress? Can you believe how fast the time has gone?

All of Lent is about preparation, evaluation, and self-examination. This is our final week of this season. That doesn't mean we are to indulge in a frenzy of self-incrimination or activity. We're certainly not to attempt accomplishing six weeks of spiritual growth in one week, but we are to take honest account of where we are and hold steady. This is no time to abandon ship just because we might not have accomplished all our goals. Remember, all of life is a process, and the journey is an end in itself.

Even so did Christ's earthly ministry come full circle. He began His ministry with the witness of a voice from heaven, "This is my beloved Son, in whom I am well pleased" (Matt. 3:17). Similarly, in the final days before His passion, Christ echoed words from the Lord's Prayer as He said, "Father, glorify thy name." Then came there a voice from heaven, saying, "I have both glorified it, and will glorify it again" (John 12:28). That same assurance with which Christ entered Holy Week can be ours.

"The kingdom, and the power, and the glory, for ever"

We began our study of the Lord's Prayer by praying, just as Christ did, that God's name would be hallowed and that His kingdom would come to earth. And here we are, full circle, ascribing the kingdom, power, and glory to Him, so that we can be part of glorifying His name.

It's little wonder, after seeing the immeasurable depth and power in the Lord's Prayer, that it should end with a great hymn of praise and recitation of our faith in God's power over all forever: What else can we possibly do but focus on the greatness of God and give Him praise and thanksgiving! The oldest manuscripts, however, do not include this final doxology. Scholars believe this was added after Jesus' resurrection. The Roman Catholic Church today often recites the prayer in this shorter form as recorded in Luke 11:2-4, without the ending praise. But I'll have to confess that I prefer the Anglican form, which adds a repetition for emphasis—"For thine is the kingdom, and the power, and the glory, for ever and ever. Amen." This is taken from the Great Bible of 1539. The King James Bible, which was published 62 years later, gave us the version with which we are most familiar—found in Matt. 6:9-13.

Our friend Charles Simeon says, "On a review of the Lord's Prayer, we cannot but be thankful that such a summary is here given us, not only because we are hereby instructed what to pray for, but are assured that, great as the petitions are, they shall all be granted, if we offer them up in faith."[2] And again, we've made a circle, for in the early days of our study we considered the propriety of forming a prayer, the heart of which was asking God for things.

To which Simeon says, "Prayer is intended to impress our own minds with a sense of our manifold necessities, and of our dependence upon God for a supply of them; and thus to prepare our souls for a grateful reception of the Divine favours: and consequently, the more urgent our prayers are, the more will these ends be answered; and God will be the more glorified by us, when he has imparted to us the desired benefits.

"As a plea, this part of the prayer admirably enforces every petition in it. Great are the things which we have asked in it: and utterly unworthy are we to offer such petitions at the throne of grace: but God is a mighty Sovereign, who 'may do what he will with his own,' and therefore may hear and answer us."[3]

Applying just the doxology to any situation can in itself be a wonderful prayer. Think of using it to pray for your children, for example: "Keep them in Your kingdom. Protect them with Your power. Let them live for Your glory." This is the prayer I have prayed for each of my four children from their earliest days—and now will be praying for my grandchildren. I can think of nothing to ask for them that isn't encompassed in this praise petition.

John Wesley expands on this thought as a summary of the prayer when he says, "Now, the principal desire of a Christian's heart being the glory of God, and all he wants for himself or his brethren being the 'daily bread' of soul and body, pardon of sin, and deliverance from the power of it and of the devil, there is nothing beside that a Christian can wish for: therefore this prayer comprehends all his desires. Eternal life is the certain consequence, or rather completion, of holiness."[4]

And, as we began by asking that God's name be made holy in all the earth and that His kingdom would truly come to earth, so we can pray the doxology for our world: "'For thine is the kingdom' (please let it be Thine; let this earthly kingdom be Yours), 'the power, and the glory' (let our generation worship and serve You in Your true power and glory; help us to give You Your rightful place in all things), 'for ever' (send a great revival that will last not for a few years only but unto the thousandth generation).

"As it was in the beginning, is now and ever shall be, world without end. Amen."

Prayer Guide
Praying the Doxology

1. As you look back over your journey through Lent what new insights have you gained?

What successes have you gained?

Have there been failures?

How can failures be turned to successes?

2. Three times in Christ's earthly ministry a voice spoke from heaven. Look up Matt. 3:17; 17:5; and John 12:28. What was the purpose of God speaking audibly in these situations?

How can we hear God's voice?

3. One way to sense God's presence is to draw near to Him in praise. A doxology, such as we are studying here, is an ascription of glory, a hymn of praise whether spoken or sung. There are many in the Bible: 1 Chron. 16:10-12, 27-29; Pss. 8:1; 24:7-10; Isa. 40:5; 58:8; 60:1-2; Luke 2:9-14; John 1:14; Rom. 11:33-36; 2 Cor. 4:6; 1 Tim. 1:17; Jude 24-25; Rev. 5:12-14; 19:1. One of the best ways to appreciate the beauty of these passages is to read them aloud. Then record some of your favorite phrases in your journal.

4. Many wonderful hymns also praise God's power and glory. Read or sing aloud "Glorious Things of Thee Are Spoken," "Joyful, Joyful, We Adore Thee," "Praise, My Soul, the King of Heaven," "Praise to the Lord, the Almighty." What aspects of God's nature do these hymns help you praise?

5. Using the form of the Lord's Prayer doxology, write a prayer invoking God's kingdom, power, and glory for some person or situation. Record this in your prayer journal.

6. God uses His power to answer our prayers to the glory of His kingdom. What answers to prayer have you seen since you began this study?

List them as your final festoon on page 22.

7. Pray now your fully festooned Lord's Prayer, saying each phrase of the

prayer and adding all the people, places, and circumstances you have listed. When you conclude, think about the fact that saying "Amen" is a way of giving full assent to all that has been said and also imparts a desire that the things that have been asked may be granted. You may, therefore, want to conclude "Amen and amen," in order to express more strongly the ardor of your desire.

PART II

Praying

the Psalms
Through
Holy Week

Ps. 118:19-29

Open to me the gates of righteousness: I will go
into them, and I will praise the Lord:
This gate of the Lord, into which the righteous
shall enter.
I will praise thee: for thou hast heard me, and art
become my salvation.
The stone which the builders refused is become the
head stone of the corner.
This is the Lord's doing; it is marvellous in our
eyes.
This is the day which the Lord hath made; we will
rejoice and be glad in it.
Save now, I beseech thee, O Lord: O Lord, I beseech thee, send now prosperity.
Blessed be he that cometh in the name of the Lord:
we have blessed you out of the house of the
Lord.
God is the Lord, which hath shewed us light: bind
the sacrifice with cords, even unto the horns
of the altar.
Thou art my God, and I will praise thee: thou art
my God, I will exalt thee.
O give thanks unto the Lord; for he is good: for
his mercy endureth for ever.

Enter His Courts with Praise: Palm Sunday

The breeze was just sufficient to make the daffodils dance. The morning sunshine highlighted the unfurling leaves on the willow trees. "Blessed is the King who comes in the name of the Lord," the vicar said.

"Peace in heaven and glory in the highest," the congregation replied.

"Assist us mercifully with your help, O Lord God of our salvation, that we may enter with joy upon the contemplation of those mighty acts, whereby you have given us life and immortality; through Jesus Christ our Lord."

And all the people said, "Amen."

It was my first Palm Sunday service, and I could hardly contain my joy at the fresh, blowing beauty of God's creation as the pastor read the scripture against the backdrop of the English Tudor church. I had attended church all my life, you understand, and I could remember being given palm branches as a child in Sunday School; but this was the first time I had experienced a service where the whole congregation participated in reenacting the events of Christ's triumphal entry into Jerusalem.

The choir, wearing angelic, pale blue robes and playing tone bells, led the procession into the church. As I followed, waving my palm branch and singing "All Glory, Laud, and Honor," I knew that Holy Week that year would have a meaning for me I'd never known before.

The week between Palm Sunday and Easter is the most important week in the Christian calendar. It has even been called "the defining week of the entire year." This one week, called the Great Week in the Early Church, and often called Passion Week today, encompasses the arrest, conviction, crucifixion, death, burial, and resurrection of Christ. "It was a week in which the world was redeemed—a week in which the re-creation of the world began."[1]

From the beginning of the Church, Christians have observed these days in special ways. The earliest pattern for an Easter celebration is those beautiful words of Paul's to the Corinthians that have become a traditional part of communion services around the world: "Christ our passover is sacrificed for us: Therefore let us keep the feast" (1 Cor. 5:7-8).

In the late fourth century a woman named Egeria made a pilgrimage from Gaul to the Holy Land. Egeria was a sharp observer and kept a meticulous journal of all she experienced. From the *Pilgrimage of Egeria* we learn a lot about early Christian worship, including her participation in the events of the Great Week in Jerusalem. And Egeria was part of a Palm Sunday procession something like the one I participated in 1,600 years later. It's no wonder my roots were tingling. Just as deep roots will make a tree stable and enable it to stand against the most violent storm, so can an awareness of the depth of the roots of our faith strengthen us against the winds of doubt.

And so through this Holy Week we will be studying the historic events of the life of Christ and the ways the Christian Church has reenacted those events for 2,000 years. At the same time we will practice one of the oldest forms of prayer—praying the Psalms.

PRAISING WITH THE PSALMS

When I was preparing to write *Glastonbury*, my epic novel on the history of Christianity in England, I spent a week in a Benedictine monastery. I loved the peace and quiet, the time to read and meditate in the cloistered garden, and the experience of praying at regular hours through the day and night with the monks. But I could never quite understand why they spent so much time praying Psalms. Of course the Psalms were beautiful and they were Holy Scripture, but weren't there 65 other books of the Bible? What was so special about the Psalms?

Then my husband gave me Thomas Merton's *Praying the Psalms* for Mother's Day, and I found that Merton began his book with my questions: Why has the Church always considered the Psalms her most perfect book of prayer? Why have the Psalms always made up the greater part of the Office recited by Christian leaders through the ages? Why, too, should the Christian layperson turn to the Psalms and make use of them in his or her own prayers to God?

Merton answers that in the Psalms we "drink divine praise at its pure and stainless source."[2] The Psalms "are the songs of men who knew who God was. If we are to pray well, we too must discover the Lord to whom we speak"[3] and praying the Psalms can help lead to the discovery of new truths of the nature of God.

The Psalms, Merton continues, "Are the songs of the whole Church, the very expression of her deepest inner life. . . . because God has given Himself to her in them, as though in a sacrament. . . . in singing the Psalms each day, the Church is therefore singing the wedding hymn of her union with God in Christ."[4] Very simply, "the Psalms are the best possible way of praising God."[5] There could be no better time to enter into this experience of praise than during the week when the whole Christian world is commemorating Christ's death and resurrection.

Now that we've seen *why* we should pray the Psalms, let us consider *how* to pray the Psalms. Although we will spend only one week of the Church calendar on this, we will learn habits and methods that will enrich our praying for the rest of our lives. First, to make the Psalms true prayers we must make the concepts expressed in the passage we are praying truly our own, by understanding what the psalmist means, then by drawing on our own experiences, thoughts, or feelings to identify in a personal way with the written words. Try to recall a time in your life when you felt the emotion the psalmist is expressing in any particular passage. The Psalms run the entire gamut of human experience: joy, rage, sorrow, exultation, depression, anger, fear, peace . . . Learn to recognize your own experiences in the psalm you are praying.

Next, remember that the Psalms are poetry—poetry written to be sung, actually. To appreciate the sound of the words, read them aloud. Or better yet, sing them. A very simple method for singing, or really, chanting the Psalms is the ancient method of singing each line on a single note, called the reciting note, then on the last 3 syllables of the line (discounting any unaccented final syllables) flex to the completing chords. (See p. 58 for melody.) Whether you prefer to read aloud, chant, or sing to a more varied melody, the point is to acquire a habit of reciting the psalm slowly and well, always thinking of the meaning of the words and allowing the Holy Spirit to pray through you.

And finally, to return once more to Thomas Merton, we are reminded that "there is no aspect of the interior life, no kind of religious experience, no spiritual need of man that is not depicted and lived out in the Psalms. But we cannot lay hands on these riches unless we are willing to work for them."[6] The work we are directed to do is to pray the Psalms with zeal and perseverance applying faith, confidence, and love. This is a matter of raising our spirit to His Spirit rather than a matter of study. Merton warns, if we approach the Psalms seeking only to "get something out of them" we will be frustrated because our efforts will be turned in the wrong direction: toward ourselves rather than toward God.

It is not what we get out of the Psalms that rewards us, but what we put into them. As we walk through the events of this Holy Week let's use the words of the psalmist to allow God to "pray in us in His own words."

Prayer Guide
Entering the Gates of Righteousness

1. Let your prayer corner reflect the fact that this is the most important week of the year. If you have a palm from a Palm Sunday service, lay it out on a table with a red cloth. Red, the special color for feast days, is especially appropriate for Palm Sunday, leading as it does to the shedding of Christ's blood, and

is a startling reminder of the deepest meaning of the season. Add a candle, Easter pictures, or flowers.

2. Read Luke 19:20-40. Record your thoughts about praise.

3. Ps. 118 is one of the great psalms of praise and adoration, which Thomas Merton calls the "Psalms par excellence. They are more truly Psalms than all the others," he says, "for the real purpose of a Psalm is to praise God."[7] Read Ps. 118:19-29 aloud. Now read it again quietly and thoughtfully. List the psalmist's reasons for praising the Lord:

Read Matt. 21:9; Mark 11:9-10; Luke 19:38; John 12:13. List the praises:

List your own reasons for praising the Lord:

4. Ps. 118 is traditionally read for Palm Sunday. Note in your journal the prophetic praise of verse 26, the messianic reference of verse 22, and the image of gates of verses 19 and 20.

5. "The gate of the Lord" is a strong image. Read Ps. 24:7-8, 10. Pss. 24 and 118 remind us of Jesus riding through the gate of Jerusalem as He entered the city, then entering the Temple gates to cast out the money changers (Matt. 21:12) at the end of His ride. The Temple gates were also the gates through which the people of the Lord entered to praise Him. How can we figuratively enter the gates of righteousness to praise the Lord?

6. Meditate on the events of Palm Sunday, trying to picture in your mind the crowds, the procession, the donkey, the disciples. What were the sounds? the smells? How would you have felt, had you been present that day? Write an entry in your prayer journal as if you were there.

7. One of the major purposes of praying the Psalms is to learn more of the nature of God. Do you need to make additions to your "aspects of God's nature I praise Him for" on page 22?

8. Now, try chanting Ps. 118. Mark each line with a flex three syllables from the end to indicate where you will change tone:

Open to me the gates of <u>righteousness</u>;

I will go into them, and I will <u>praise</u> the Lord.

This is an Anglican chant, an offspring of metrical psalm-singing, not plainsong or Gregorian chant, which is much older. This is a double chant, that is, there are melody lines for two lines of psalm. The first chord repeats for the entire line, then shifts according to your flex markings.

Ps. 142

I cried unto the LORD with my voice; with my
    voice unto the LORD did I make my sup-
    plication.
I poured out my complaint before him; I
    shewed before him my trouble.
When my spirit was overwhelmed within me,
    then thou knewest my path. In the way
    wherein I walked have they privily laid a
    snare for me.
I looked on my right hand, and beheld, but
    there was no man that would know me:
    refuge failed me; no man cared for my
    soul.
I cried unto thee, O LORD: I said, Thou art my
    refuge and my portion in the land of the
    living.
Attend unto my cry; for I am brought very
    low: deliver me from my persecutors; for
    they are stronger than I.
Bring my soul out of prison, that I may praise
    thy name: the righteous shall compass
    me about; for thou shalt deal bountifully
    with me.

9

From Trouble to Triumph: Maundy Thursday

I am constantly amazed at the power of story. Stories are what identify a nation or a family. When you want to get acquainted with a person, one of the most important ways to do so is to learn his or her story. A person's, family's, or nation's self-image is based on their story, and keeping that story alive by retelling it is essential to their survival.

One of the things that distinguishes Christianity from most other religions is the fact that ours is not a philosophy or an ethical system, but a history. Because this story is the central fact of all human history and of our lives, one of the most important things we can do when we gather is to reenact these historical events. Through the 2,000 years since Jesus Christ lived, died, and rose again, His followers have developed meaningful ways of telling His story. That retelling is what Holy Week services are all about.

From earliest times Maundy Thursday, the Thursday of Holy Week, was a day of special solemnity. It was originally marked by ceremonial bathing of the candidates who were to be baptized on Easter eve. Gradually the ceremony was changed into foot washing. In medieval times the king washed the feet of one beggar for each year of his life, then gave specially minted "Maundy Money" to the poor. The name Maundy comes from the Latin *mandatum* (commandment) because John 13:34 ("A new commandment I give unto you, That ye love one another") was sung at early foot-washing ceremonies, as it often is today.

Robert Webber says, "In the ancient church the service of Maundy Thursday began the great triduum, the three great days of the paschal celebration. These were days of fasting and prayer, days when the church remembered the final acts of Christ's saving work."[1]

In medieval times Holy Week services began on Wednesday, sometimes called Spy Wednesday as a reference to Judas spying on Jesus (John 13:2). The service was called Tenebrae, which is Latin for "darkness." As the sufferings and death of Christ were recounted in the chants, each candle was extinguished, leaving the church in tomblike darkness. At the end of the service the worshipers left in silence. This must have been enormously effective in the bone-chilling cold of a vast cathedral as the footsteps echoed hollowly on the stone floor.

By the 18th century the services were less dramatic, but still effective. John Wesley recounted in his journal the Maundy Thursday experience of a young woman named Frances Fugate: "I was now more and more convinced that I was a guilty, undone sinner. I cried to God day and night, laying down my work many times in a day. On Holy-Thursday, 1756, I was sadly afraid of going to the sacrament. However, I broke through and went. At the Lord's table I found such a love as I cannot express."[2]

Today, Maundy Thursday services still reenact the events of Thursday of the first Holy Week: Christ instituted the Lord's Supper, He washed His disciples' feet, and He went out into the Garden of Gethsemane to pray. Participating in these re-creations can help us remember what Christ did in earning our salvation and in a small way help us enter into the experience. A traditional Holy Thursday service begins with Communion, then a foot washing ceremony, followed by an all-night prayer vigil.

The *Book of Common Prayer* instructs the leader at a foot washing to say: "The Lord Jesus, after he had supped with his disciples and had washed their feet, said to them, 'Do you know what I, your Lord and master, have done to you? I have given you an example, that you should do as I have done.'"

Webber says, "When we celebrate this service, we renew the covenant between God and ourselves, and we are made ready for his death and resurrection."[3]

PRAYING WHEN YOU'RE OVERWHELMED

Ps. 143 is a lament written by David when he was hiding in a cave, fleeing the wrath of King Saul who wanted to kill him. Now you may have faced some pretty dire circumstances. You might even be facing some now. But not many of us have had to hide in a cave because the king wanted to kill us. So right there we can take a sort of negative comfort from praying this psalm: No matter how bad things are, they could be worse.

But seriously, a lament is an expression of profound grief, of passionate mourning over a loss, or the bewailing of an occurrence. Lamenting is something we hope not to have to do too much of in this life, but we know that such times are part of life. And when they come we can know that King David and Jesus Christ have been in such circumstances before us and we have their words and examples to help us through, as well as the living presence of Christ.

David was concentrating on his own circumstances when he wrote this heart-cry to the Lord. He did not realize he was also writing a messianic psalm. But as we meditate on Ps. 142 and think of the events that Christ faced on Maundy Thursday, we can see how David's experience prefigured that of Christ's. David was hiding in a cave. Christ's body would be laid in a cave. David's enemies had set a trap for him. Jesus' enemies set a trap for Him. David's spirit was overwhelmed. Christ sweat drops of blood in the garden. David found no one that knew him. The disciples deserted and denied Jesus. David cried, "Deliver me from my persecutors." Jesus prayed, "Let this cup pass from me."

David was brought out of the cave for a fruitful earthly reign. Christ was brought out of the grave for a triumphant heavenly reign. And so the psalm ends in comfort, "The righteous shall compass me about; for thou shalt deal bountifully with me." And so can we look forward to being brought out of our troubles. Righteous friends will surround us, and God will deal generously with us.

Prayer Guide
Praying When We Have Complaints

1. Read 1 Sam. 19:8-11; 20:1; 22:1. Then read Ps. 142 aloud, from David's viewpoint. What images did you picture?

Read Matt. 26:36-50. Now read Ps. 142 aloud, from Christ's viewpoint. What images came to mind?

Think of your present problems or remember a time when you were in distress. Pray Ps. 142 aloud for yourself. What do you picture? Record your images in your journal.

2. Notice that the psalmist says twice that he will cry unto the Lord with his voice. What difference do you notice when you pray aloud compared to silent prayer?

3. One thing this psalm teaches is "the blessedness and comfort of telling one's troubles to God; a fearless, intimate intercourse with God is a means of union with him."[4] Taking our complaints to God is the proper thing to do with them. List your complaints.

Take them to God.

4. The psalmist cries for deliverance from his persecutors. Most of us don't have persecutors, but we have people who irritate and trouble us. Name them.

Talk to God about them.

5. Although all his friends have deserted him for the moment and he felt no one cared for his soul, the psalmist looks forward confidently to being surrounded and comforted by righteous friends. List your Christian friends.

Thank God for them.

6. Notice that even when he was overwhelmed, the psalmist was confident that God knew his path (v. 3). God not only knows but also cares. List the Bible references you can think of that tell of God's eye on us and His caring for us.

7. Notice that David wanted to be delivered from prison (actually, asked that his soul be released—which implies a spiritual, rather than a physical release) "that I may praise thy name." What can we learn from this example?

8. Ps. 57 was also written by David when he was hiding from Saul in the cave. Read this psalm and compare to Ps. 142.

9. Chant Ps. 142 to experience its full impact.

Ps. 22:1-21 (KJV)

My God, my God, why hast thou forsaken me? why art thou so far from
    helping me, and from the words of my roaring?

O my God, I cry in the daytime, but thou hearest not; and in the night sea-
    son, and am not silent.

But thou art holy, O thou that inhabitest the praises of Israel.

Our fathers trusted in thee: they trusted, and thou didst deliver them.

They cried unto thee, and were delivered: they trusted in thee, and were not
    confounded.

But I am a worm, and no man; a reproach of men, and despised of the peo-
    ple.

All they that see me laugh me to scorn: they shoot out the lip, they shake the
    head, saying,

He trusted on the LORD that he would deliver him: let him deliver him, see-
    ing he delighted in him.

But thou art he that took me out of the womb: thou didst make me hope
    when I was upon my mother's breasts.

I was cast upon thee from the womb: thou art my God from my mother's
    belly.

Be not far from me; for trouble is near; for there is none to help.

Many bulls have compassed me: strong bulls of Bashan have beset me
    round.

They gaped upon me with their mouths, as a ravening and a roaring lion.

I am poured out like water, and all my bones are out of joint: my heart is
    like wax; it is melted in the midst of my bowels.

My strength is dried up like a potsherd; and my tongue cleaveth to my
    jaws; and thou hast brought me into the dust of death.

For dogs have compassed me: the assembly of the wicked have inclosed me:
    they pierced my hands and my feet.

I may tell all my bones: they look and stare upon me.

They part my garments among them, and cast lots upon my vesture.

But be not thou far from me, O LORD: O my strength, haste thee to help me.

Deliver my soul from the sword; my darling from the power of the dog.

Save me from the lion's mouth: for thou hast heard me from the horns of the
    unicorns.

The Dark Night of the Soul: Good Friday

All day the court fasted, each alone in his room, no one speaking, wearing nothing but black. Church bells rang a dull, muffled clang as their metal clappers had been replaced by wooden ones—for no peal of joy could be heard on this day. On the table in the king's hall a single piece of meat was set out to grow worm-eaten and maggoty—a reminder of the end that awaits all mortal flesh.

Good Friday at the court of King Henry VIII—the first Good Friday in the newly established Church of England—was a day of tension beyond the usual spiritual significance of the day. How would this holy day be celebrated by the king who had made himself head of a new church and taken for his queen one whom the people called the great whore?

At last the hour arrived. Three o'clock, the hour of Satan's triumph. All gathered in the silent blackness of the abbey. First came two priests of the new persuasion wearing their plain white collars rather than the rich vestments of the Roman faith, carrying lighted candles. Right behind them Archbishop Thomas Cranmer carried a veiled cross. At the altar he lifted the veil. "This is the cross on which hung the Salvation of the world."

"Come, let us worship," the congregation responded. Then all knelt in silence. Accompanied by the candle-bearing priests, the archbishop carried the cross the full length of the great nave and placed it on the cold stone surface of the sanctuary entrance, flanked by the two candles. No heads turned, but every eye looked sideways to see what King Henry would do next. All the court had heard the rumor that Anne had laughed at the traditional procession of creeping to the cross on one's knees. But Henry had not laughed. The priests began the antiphon. "We worship Thee. Lord, we venerate Thy cross. We praise Thy resurrection. Through the cross Thou hast brought joy to the world."

Henry, wearing only a pair of thin black hose over the royal knees, led forth up the long nave on his knees, his eyes never wavering from the cross.

Fortunately, Good Friday services are considerably less grueling to-day. Good Friday, or "God's Friday," is the day on which God reconciled the world to himself through Christ's death on the Cross. Second to Easter itself, it is the most important day in the Christian calendar and a day on which many churches hold significant services of remembrance.

In the primitive Church the special feature of Good Friday was the fast in preparation for the baptismal service that would take place be-fore the Easter Eucharist. The fast is mentioned as early as A.D. 50-150 in the *Didache.* Tertullian says that the reason for fasting was that the Bridegroom is taken away. There was no celebration of the Eucharist on this day, but by the 8th century a special service had developed where the faithful partook of previously consecrated elements. Other types of services that were observed as early as the 4th century in Jerusalem in-cluded a mimetic representation of our Lord's experiences in the way of the Cross, the veneration of the Cross, and even a three hours' service of readings, hymns, and preaching.

In the 18th century John Wesley was careful to observe Good Friday, recording the events of the day specifically in his journal on 27 occa-sions. He mentions going to church, then preaching—up to four times a day—holding Communion services, covenant services, and watch night services as Good Friday observances. His experiences of April 1, 1743, sound even more grueling than those of Henry VIII: "Being Good-Friday, between seven and eight I set out with John Heally, my guide. The north wind being unusually high, drove the sleet in our face, which froze as it fell, and cased us over presently. When we came to Placey, we could very hardly stand. As soon as we were a little recovered, I went into the Square, and declared Him who 'was wounded for our transgressions,' and 'bruised for our iniquities.' The poor sinners were quickly gathered together, and gave earnest heed to the things which were spoken."

Three years later Wesley, at the age of 82, hastened 24 miles by horseback through the sharpest frost he said he had ever known to con-duct a Good Friday service in Birmingham. "But indeed our House was hot enough in the evening; and I have not seen a more earnest people."

Today the two most typical Good Friday services are the stations of the cross and services of solemn prayers. A typical stations of the cross service for today is found in *The Biblical Way of the Cross* by Michael Dubruiel and Amy Welborn. Either in a church or out of doors, 14 sta-tions are set up to symbolize Christ's progress to the Cross. If possible, the people follow the leader from station to station. The leader names each station and says, "We praise you, Jesus, and give you thanks!" The people respond, "By your cross and resurrection you have set us free!" A scripture reading follows and then the people kneel for prayer. Before moving on to the next station, leader and people repeat the traditional kyrie: "Lord, have mercy." "Christ, have mercy." "Lord, have mercy." The meditation on each station is usually interspersed with music.

The service of solemn prayers has come down to us from the more elaborate medieval form of the veneration of the Cross—but with no creeping to the cross on our knees as Henry VIII underwent. In this service, usually held at noon, the congregation enters in silence and kneels in a church stripped of all ornamentation. The ministers enter also in silence, usually wearing black robes. The service proceeds through Bible readings, prayers, and a sermon. If hymns are sung, they are in a minor key. Prayers particularly focus on those who suffer and those who have not received the gospel of Christ. Communion may be served from previously consecrated elements. The service concludes with a prayer such as the one given in the *Book of Common Prayer:* "Lord Jesus Christ, son of the living God, we pray you to set your passion, cross, and death between your judgment and our souls, now and in the hour of our death. Give mercy and grace to the living; pardon and rest to the dead; to your holy Church peace and concord; and to us sinners everlasting life and glory; for with the Father and the Holy Spirit you live and reign, one God, now and for ever. Amen." The congregation departs in silence.

Unlike Christmas and Easter, Good Friday is not generally recognized in today's society. Even many Christian churches do not hold special services. Extra effort is required to observe this holy day. Good Friday was never a vacation day when my children were in school, but I often took them out of classes at noon so we could attend special services. I felt rewarded this year when, in spite of military and college schedules, they made time in their lives to commemorate our Lord's sacrifice of himself for our sins.

PRAYING WHEN YOU FEEL FORSAKEN

I took my baby to the doctor for her eighth-month checkup. "Doctor, when do babies start sleeping through the night?" (This was my fourth child—you'd think I'd have known by then!) Dr. Copple looked me up and down. "So that's why your eyes are so red. Let her cry it out—it won't hurt her."

Right. It probably didn't hurt her; but it hurt me. I took the question to my friend who was pregnant with her 10th child. (Yes, 10th!) "What do you do, Saundra?"

"I get up with them. You know, you don't really lose that much sleep and sometimes that's the only time I have in the whole day to be alone with that baby and cuddle it. But you can spoil them. I did that with Travis. He was getting me up at 5:30 every morning for a playtime. It was my fault, but he had to suffer for it when it came time that we had to cry it out.

"I lay in the next room listening to him and cried right along with him. But you know, the Lord showed me something really special—Travis didn't know I was in the next room suffering with him, but I was.

Sometimes I don't know where God is when I have a problem, but He's right in the next room crying with me."

And so must God the Father have cried when His Son was alone on the Cross, abandoned to our sins. But God was faithful. Easter morning followed Good Friday. Morning sunrise follows the dark of midnight. Springtime flowers burst forth after the coldest winter. God is always faithful. No matter what despair we may experience, we can rely on God's faithfulness.

I find John Wesley's notes on Ps. 22 especially enlightening: "'My God—who are my friend and father, though now thou frownest upon me, I am forsaken—you have withdrawn the light of thy countenance, the supports and comforts of thy spirit, and filled me with the terrors of thy wrath.

"'But thou art just and true in all thy ways.' This he adds to strengthen his faith, and to enforce his prayers, and prevail with God for the honour of his holy name, to hear and help him."[1]

Although this psalm presents a picture of deep suffering—the deepest ever endured on earth—the theme of the psalm is God's faithfulness. Indeed, this faithfulness is revealed in the very words of this cry of desperation, because the prophecies not only declared what works our Lord would do and what sufferings He would endure, but even the very words He would utter. God was faithful in the fulfillment of His revelation.

And it's important that we realize that even in this darkest, most extreme hour of His suffering, Jesus did not lose confidence in God. Charles Simeon says that in this Christ "exhibited the brightest pattern to all his tempted people. Not for one moment does Jesus doubt his relation to his heavenly Father, as we alas! are too apt to do in seasons of deep affliction. His repetition of that endearing name, 'My God! my God!' shews how steadfastly he maintained his faith and confidence; and teaches us, that 'when we are walking in darkness and have no light, we should trust in the Lord, and stay ourselves upon our God.'"[2]

And so we can pray this psalm with David and with Christ, knowing that the light will come. When I was going through a particularly difficult time a few years ago I didn't really mind how long the tunnel was—I just wanted assurance that it was a tunnel, not a hole. But the light was there—even when I couldn't see it—as it always is because the Light of the World never fails.

Prayer Guide
Praying with Assurance of God's Faithfulness

1. Christ on the Cross drew strength from His confidence in the nature of God, "But thou art holy." The holiness of God is a major emphasis of the Old Testament, as the love of God is a major emphasis of the New Testament. We can always be confident in the nature of God because it is unchangeable from age to age. Name some of the aspects of God's nature in which you place the most confidence.

2. Even in the despair of the Cross Christ found comfort in recalling God's saving acts in history (vv. 5-6). Recount some of His saving acts in scripture and in the history of the world.

3. In verses 9 and 10 Christ draws strength from recalling God's faithfulness in His own life. Recount examples of God's faithfulness in your life.

4. "They shoot out their lip" and "they shake their head" refers to the derision of the crowd around the Cross. It is fulfilled in Matt. 27:41-43. Have you been mocked unfairly at some time?

How did you get through it?

5. Ps. 22 is the beginning of a trilogy of psalms: 22, "Christ the Saviour"; 23, "Christ the Shepherd"; 24, "Christ the Sovereign"[3] Read all three. What strength do you draw from this progression?

6. Ps. 22 is often compared to Ps. 69. Read it. What similarities do you find?

7. Ps. 22 is also linked with Isa. 53, which is some of the most magnificent poetry every written. How do the words of Isaiah help deepen your devotion to Jesus Christ?

8. Our cutting of Ps. 22 is left on a solemn note rather than going on to the words of praise and deliverance with which it ends (especially vv. 25-27) because this is Good Friday. Christ is still in the tomb. The world is in mourning. We must wait for the glory of Easter. We live in a world that demands instant gratification. Waiting is not popular. What is the value of learning to wait?

9. Chant Ps. 22:1-21.

Ps. 130

Out of the depths have I cried unto thee, O
    LORD.
Lord, hear my voice: let thine ears be attentive
    to the voice of my supplications.
If thou, LORD, shouldest mark iniquities, O
    Lord, who shall stand?
But there is forgiveness with thee, that thou
    mayest be feared.
I wait for the LORD, my soul doth wait, and in
    his word do I hope.
My soul waiteth for the Lord more than they
    that watch for the morning: I say, more
    than they that watch for the morning.
Let Israel hope in the LORD: for with the LORD
    there is mercy, and with him is plenteous
    redemption.
And he shall redeem Israel from all his iniqui-
    ties.

Expectancy: Easter Eve

N o! You must not be lighting the fire tonight!"
Patrick, missionary to this wild, pagan land faced his guide. "This is the eve of the dawning of God's salvation. The Paschal fire celebrates the victory of the Light of the world over eternal darkness."

"Yes, yes, light a fire. But not tonight. You must not. In all of Ireland there are no fires on this one night of the year."

"And why is that?"

"Tomorrow is the high king's birthday. All fires save the king's feast-fire are to be cold tonight until the high king himself lights the first one in the morning. Then all will have the lighting of their fires in honor of the day that gave our king birth."

"We will light our fire first in honor of the day that God gave the new birth to mankind."

"But it is a dying matter to disobey the king in this. You will be put to death."

Patrick had no desire that his mission to Christianize Ireland should so end before it began, but he would not fail to honor God on this, the holiest night of the year. He directed his fellow missionaries to build a great bonfire atop the hill of Slane, in full view of Tara where the high king feasted. When the fire blazed high he stretched out his arms. "You, O Christ, are the Light of the world. A light on a hill cannot be hidden. We ask that this, our paschal fire will shed light among all those in this, our new land, so that they may come to know and glorify our Father in heaven."

Patrick took the small loaf of bread one of his fellows held. He blessed it, broke it in half, and held it up to be illuminated by the leaping flames. "The body of Christ. Our Lord said, 'This is my body.' We also are His body. So may we go out to do His work."

St. Patrick's was not the first paschal fire, but it was certainly the most dramatic, followed as it was by his arrest and being drug, bound, before the high king of Ireland—an opportunity the missionary used to preach the gospel of salvation.

Today the celebration is called the great vigil of Easter and begins with these words in the *Book of Common Prayer:* "Dear friends in Christ: On this most holy night, in which our Lord Jesus passed over from death to life, the Church invites her members, dispersed throughout the World, to gather in vigil and prayer. For this is the Passover of the Lord, in which, by hearing his Word and celebrating his Sacraments, we share in his victory over death."

The feast of the resurrection of Christ is the greatest and oldest feast of the Christian Church. From the 2nd century the celebration of Easter Sunday began with a lengthy vigil on Holy Saturday and included baptism at cockcrow followed by the Eucharist. A church order from early in the third century directs worshipers to, "Watch all night in prayers, supplications, the reading of the prophets, of the Gospel and of psalms in fear and trembling and continual supplication until three in the morning."

In the early 4th century Augustine called this vigil "the mother of all vigils." At that time the vigil included a sermon and the whole history of salvation was recounted in readings and songs. The vigil culminated in the joyous celebration of the Eucharist after midnight. The lighting of the paschal candle and the baptism of new Christians gradually became features of the vigil as well.

We find the observance still alive and well in 18th-century England. In his journal John Wesley records his devout observance of Easter, beginning with his defense of the practice of holding vigils in his reply to a critic who had charged him with holding "midnight assemblies." "Sir," Wesley replied, "did you never see the word Vigil in your Common-Prayer Book? Do you know what it means? If not, permit me to tell you, that it was customary with the ancient Christians to spend whole nights in prayer; and that these nights were termed Vigiliæ, or Vigils. Therefore for spending a part of some nights in this manner, in public and solemn prayer, we have not only the authority of our own national Church, but of the universal Church, in the earliest ages."[1]

Likewise Wesley records numerous early morning Easter services, such as: "We met at four in the morning, on Easter-day, (1745) and great was our joy in the Lord." And again, in 1760, more than 1,200 years after St. Patrick, "I never saw more numerous or more serious congregations in Ireland than we had all this week. On Easter-Day, April 6, I introduced our English custom, beginning the service at four in the morning."

Although modern congregations choose to meet at more congenial hours, the paschal vigil continues today in many churches to reflect the basic pattern of the worship of the early centuries of Christendom: The celebrant kindles a new fire outside the church, symbolizing the resurrection of the Light of the World. The paschal candle is lighted from this fire and is carried into the darkened church. Candles held by members of the congregation are lit from the paschal candle and lights are turned on in the church. Now the church bells, which have been silenced since Maundy Thursday, peal forth in joy, and "Alleluia!" which has not been spoken in the church since the beginning of Lent, can again be proclaimed.

It is truly right and good, always and everywhere, with our whole heart and mind and voice, to praise you, the invisible, almighty, and eternal God, and your only-begotten Son, Jesus Christ our Lord: for he is the true Paschal Lamb, who at the feast of the Passover paid for us the debt of Adam's sin, and by his blood delivered your faithful people. . . . This is the night when you brought our fathers, the children of Israel out of bondage in Egypt. . . . This is the night when all who believe in Christ are delivered from the gloom of sin, and are restored to grace and holiness of life. . . . This is the night when Christ broke the bonds of death and hell, and rose victorious from the grave.

And so continues the service in the *Book of Common Prayer.* Scriptural readings—recounting the entire work of God in the world from creation through redemption—are interspersed with responsorial psalms, hymns, and periods of silence. A sermon, renewal of baptismal vows, the baptism of new members, and Holy Communion follow.

The paschal vigil is especially important in Russia where the faithful take their Easter eggs and special cakes called kulich to church with them for a blessing. Worshipers leave the church carrying lighted candles and parade around the building three times led by the priests and choir. At the conclusion of the procession the priest proclaims, "Christ is risen!" and the congregation responds, "He is risen indeed!"

ON THE VERGE

We saw the psalmist waiting in both Ps. 142 and Ps. 22, and in Ps. 130 he says, "I wait for the LORD" (v. 5). But the difference here is his expectant attitude. He is still in the cave, "Out of the depths have I cried unto thee, O LORD" (v. 1), but he is at the very mouth of the cave, peering into the misty gray of predawn, knowing that the sunrise is coming. And he waits with an assurance surpassing "they that watch for the morning" (v. 6).

How can he be so certain even while the world is still dark? Because "in his word do I hope" (v. 5). Our hope is not vague wishing but a firm faith grounded in the Word of God. The faithfulness of God is our rock. Our assurance is that the Lord will come with His mercy and His "plenteous redemption" (v. 7).

It may at first strike us as odd that, in the midst of all this confident expectancy in the sunrise, David says that God "mayest be feared" (see v. 4). But the very fact that God is worthy of our fear (awe, respect) as well as of our love is in itself a cause for confidence. Charles Simeon says, "Hope in God, as men generally use the term, is nothing more than an unfounded expectation that God will save us, whatever be our state, and whatever be our conduct. But a scriptural hope implies a suitable regard to the things we hope for, and to him in whom our hope is placed. It implies that we pray to him with fervour; that we wait for him with patience, that we depend on him with steadfastness. If we look inward, we shall find nothing but discouragement. But if, with David, (or with Christ in the tomb,) we look to God we may find abundant encouragement: in His attributes, in His works, and in His word."[2]

Prayer Guide
Praying in Certain Hope

1. Not many of us have our faith tested as severely as St. Patrick or as David did, but we all have times when it would be easier to go along with the crowd rather than saying, "No, I believe, so I shall do." Recount some such time in your life.

What were the results?

2. As in Ps. 142 the psalmist here refers to praying aloud, "Lord, hear my voice" (v. 2). Pray this psalm silently, then aloud. Then chant it. What differences did you find in the experience? Which did you prefer? Why?

3. The psalmist does not appeal for redemption on the basis of justice, but of mercy. One of my favorite speeches in all of Shakespeare's works is in "Measure for Measure" where the nun Isabella pleads to a harsh, legalistic ruler for her brother's life, basing her argument on the mercy of God: "Alas! Alas! Why, all the souls that were forfeit once; And He that might the vantage best have took found out the remedy. How would you be if He, which is the top of judgment, should but judge you as you are: O think on that; and mercy then will breathe within your lips like man new made." How can we apply God's mercy to others?

4. Commenting on verse 7 of Ps. 130, John Wesley said, "This mercy is the foundation of all religion." Do you agree? Why or why not?

5. Verses 5 and 6 tell us to wait for the Lord. Waiting is not my favorite thing to do. Read: Ps. 25:3-5; 27:13-14; 37:7-9, 34; Isa. 30:18; 40:31; Lam. 3:26; Mic. 7:7; Rom. 8:25. What can we learn from these?

6. Some of the key words of this Psalm are: "faithfulness," "forgiveness," "mercy," "redemption." Take these or other words that seem key to you and write a prayer, poem, or meditation on Ps. 130 in your journal.

Ps. 30

I will extol thee, O Lord; for thou hast lifted me up, and
hast not made my foes to rejoice over me.

O Lord my God, I cried unto thee, and thou hast healed
me.

O Lord, thou hast brought up my soul from the grave:
thou hast kept me alive, that I should not go down
to the pit.

Sing unto the Lord, O ye saints of his, and give thanks at
the remembrance of his holiness.

For his anger endureth but a moment; in his favour is life:
weeping may endure for a night, but joy cometh in
the morning.

And in my prosperity I said, I shall never be moved.

Lord, by thy favour thou hast made my mountain to
stand strong: thou didst hide thy face, and I was
troubled.

I cried to thee, O Lord; and unto the Lord I made supplication.

What profit is there in my blood, when I go down to the
pit? Shall the dust praise thee? shall it declare thy
truth?

Hear, O Lord, and have mercy upon me: Lord, be thou
my helper.

Thou hast turned for me my mourning into dancing: thou
hast put off my sackcloth, and girded me with gladness;

To the end that my glory may sing praise to thee, and not
be silent. O Lord my God, I will give thanks unto
thee for ever.

Joy in the Morning:
Easter Sunday

It was a crisp Easter dawning in the monastery. Somewhere in Europe. Sometime in the 11th century. The chant of the second lesson began. A brother, vested in a simple white alb, entered as if to take part in the service. Only when he sat quietly beside the altar did anyone notice that he carried a palm branch.

When the response began, three more brothers entered vested more finely in ceremonial choir habits bearing pots of burning incense, looking about as if searching for something. The white-robed brother saw them and sang forth in a sweet voice of medium pitch. "Quem Queritas?" ("Whom do you seek?")

The three replied in unison, "Jesus of Nazareth."

"He is not here. He has risen as He said. Behold now that he has risen from the dead."

The three turned and looked. "Alleluia! The Lord is risen!"

"Come and see the place." The monk enacting the angel rose and lifted the veil that should have been covering the cross. But only the cloths in which the cross was wrapped lay there.

The three seekers set their incense down, picked up the empty cloths, and sang the anthem "The Lord Has Risen from the Tomb."

Now the entire congregation took up the hymn "Te Deum Laudamus" ("We Praise You, O Lord").

And so, not only was Christ's resurrection celebrated in a new way, but also Western drama was born. For some time bits of musical dialogue had been incorporated into the celebration of Holy Communion at Christmas and Easter—a natural enough thing to do since Communion itself is a reenactment. But here, at this Easter matins service the brothers had discovered a whole new way to present the gospel to those unskilled in Latin. And amazingly, the actual texts have been preserved for us.

Today, Christians around the world still celebrate with drama and ceremony, proclaiming: The waiting is over! The first day of the week has come—the first day of a world in which living above sin in the glorious freedom of Christ's victory over death and Satan is now possible. In all churches around the world bells peal and alleluias ring.

The fact that the feast of the resurrection of Christ is the greatest and oldest feast of the Christian Church is emphasized by the long preparation of Lent and the special ceremonies of Holy Week. In the ancient church the new Christians, after watching all Saturday night, were baptized early on Easter Day and received Communion. On the night before Easter churches and even whole cities were illuminated.

The week after Easter Sunday is Easter Week, or the octave. An octave is the eighth day following a feast and includes the days in between during which the observance of the feast continues. For example, the *Book of Common Prayer* provides a special collect for each day of the week, and in Canada Easter Monday is a holiday. Hence, the Sunday after Easter is Easter octave. The practice began in the fourth century under Constantine when Easter was the first feast to be dignified with an octave. The practice probably came from the Old Testament usage of an eighth-day celebration of the Feast of Tabernacles and the dedication of the Temple.

John Wesley regularly recorded his Easter Day and Easter Week observances, giving us a good picture of the practice of Methodist societies at that time: On Easter in 1776 Wesley was obliged to preach out of doors because he found a congregation of "thousands upon thousands flocking together." He exhorted the multitude to "live unto Him who died for them and rose again."[1] During the octave the following year he "administered the Lord's Supper every morning, after the example of the Primitive Church."[2]

On Easter, March 31, 1782, he preached in the church, morning and evening, "where we had about eight hundred communicants. In the evening, we had a love-feast; and such an one as I had not seen for many years,"[3] and in 1784, when Wesley was 81 years old, he recorded preaching twice, the second service to "near a thousand communicants. But hitherto the Lord has helped me in this respect also: I have found no congregation which my voice could not command."[4] And his voice was still strong on April 4, 1790, when he was 87. "(Being Easter-day.) I think we had about one thousand six hundred communicants. I preached, both morning and evening, without weariness; and in the evening lay down in peace."[5]

Amid the flurry of Easter egg hunts, cantatas, new dresses, and family dinners that mark the season today, it's good to contemplate such focus on the central meaning of Easter. As the collect of the day from the *Book of Common Prayer* reminds us as well: "Almighty God, who through thine only-begotten Son Jesus Christ hast overcome death and opened unto us the gate of everlasting life: Grant that we, who celebrate with joy the day of the Lord's resurrection, may be raised from the death of sin by the life-giving Spirit; through the same Jesus Christ our Lord, who liveth and reigneth with thee and the same Spirit ever, one God, world without end. Amen."[6]

A SONG OF REMEMBRANCE

The three previous psalms we have studied have been the psalmist's cries of desperation from cave and tomb. Here, in Ps. 30 we have the Lord's answer: "O LORD my God, I cried unto thee; and thou hast healed me. O LORD, thou hast brought up my soul from the grave" (vv. 2-3). And so we see in the life of King David and in the life of our Lord, as we have seen in our own lives, that "weeping may endure for a night, but joy cometh in the morning" (v. 5).

In this psalm the poet sets out the meaning of life—our purpose for living: to praise and glorify God. First, the psalmist uses this as a logical argument for the reason God should keep him alive: "Shall the dust praise thee?" (v. 9). And then when God hears and grants his prayer the psalmist recounts that his mourning was turned into dancing to the end that he might "sing praise to thee, and not be silent" (v. 12). We have noted repeatedly the emphasis on voicing these prayers aloud, now we are reminded that it is likewise important to praise aloud, "and not be silent." David had probably been delivered from a very serious illness when he wrote this psalm, and when he says, "I will extol thee, O LORD; for thou hast lifted me up" (v. 1), the reference is most likely to rising from a sickbed. But, especially as we read this psalm in the Easter season, I cannot help but relate the lifting up reference to John 3:14, 8:28, and 12:32-33, where each time Jesus used the same phrase to refer to His being raised up on the Cross. When we apply that meaning, the whole psalm becomes messianic.

Whether we read the psalm from David's, Christ's, or our own viewpoint, however, it is clear that this psalm is about remembering. Our confidence and our praise are grounded in remembrance. In verse 4 we are called to remember His holiness. The holiness of God is used in the Old Testament as a summary of His nature. It would include His mercy and faithfulness and His radiant purity as well.[7] As we saw when studying the Lord's Prayer, we should always begin our prayer by remembering and praising God for himself.

Then David recalls specific instances in his own life for which he gives praise: the Lord had not allowed the king's foes to rejoice over him, God had healed him, He had kept him alive, God's anger was brief, his favour lifelong, God had made his mountain (kingdom) strong, God did not hide His face in trouble, David's mourning had been turned into dancing, He had clothed David with gladness. What a list! With such goodness showered upon him, it's little wonder that David became the greatest singer of praises to God of all time. But then, couldn't each one of us make a similar list?

Prayer Guide
Praying in the Joy of Resurrection

This is a truly worshipful psalm. It is about remembering, and the central purpose of worship is to recall God's saving deeds and promises—which is most appropriate at Easter. At Easter we are called to "hear the record of God's saving deeds in history, how he saved his people in ages past" to the purpose that each of us will be brought "to the fullness of redemption."[8] Let us review God's saving acts:

1. Read Gen. 1:1—2:2. How can we see God's saving hand in creation?

2. Read Gen. 7:1-5, 11-18; 8:6-18; 9:8-13. How can we apply God's faithfulness to Noah to ourselves?

God's covenant with Noah was a promise of His mercy. To whom? For how long?

3. Read Gen. 22:1-18. This story, prefiguring the sacrifice of Christ, ends with a promise. State it.

4. Read Exod. 14:10—15:1. How can recalling this story strengthen our faith and cause us to praise?

5. Read Isa. 4:2-6. How did God promise His presence in a renewed Israel?

6. Read Isa. 55:1-13. To whom does God offer salvation in this beautiful passage?

7. Read Ezek. 36:24-28. How is the Easter covenant of reconciliation prefigured in this passage?

8. Read Ezek. 37:1-14. How can our witnessing to God's acts and promises help give life?

9. Read Zeph. 3:12-20. Verse 12 begins with "an afflicted and poor people." By verse 20 they are "a name and a praise among all people of the earth." What brings about such a change?

10. In Ps. 30 David says God has restored him to health "to the end that my glory [tongue or soul] may sing praise to thee." List your praises.

11. Praise God by chanting Ps. 30.

Looking Ahead

For the next seven weeks until Pentecost we are in the church season of Easter, or Eastertide. The special holiness and rejoicing of this season are marked by the use of the liturgical color white, which in many churches is reserved solely for the seasons following Lent and Advent. We are leaving Easter Week, and yet, as Christians, we never leave the Easter season. We should remember that we are "Easter people" and live all year in the glow of Christ's sacrifice and resurrection.

Continuing with our praying of the Psalms can help us carry Easter forward with us. Apply the techniques we have been using through our study of Holy Week as you pray psalms for Eastertide in your private devotions.

First Sunday after Easter: Ps. 111 is a wonderful psalm for praising the Lord for all His works and His trustworthiness. It's especially appropriate following the Easter feast, as verse 5 refers to His giving meat and verse 9 praises Him for His redemption and His covenant. Sing the hymn "O Worship the King, All Glorious Above," and note the references to His saving acts.

Second Sunday after Easter: Ps. 116 is a song of personal testimony. As you pray this psalm, note how many of the statements beginning with personal pronouns you can apply to yourself. Continue your personal testimony as you sing "I Come with Joy to Meet My Saviour."

Third Sunday after Easter: Christ, the Good Shepherd, is the theme for this day in the church year. The 23rd psalm is appointed to be read, and the Gospels reading is the parable from John 10 where Christ says, "I am the door of the sheep." As you pray this beloved psalm this week conclude each prayer with the collect from the *Book of Common Prayer*: "O God, whose Son Jesus is the good shepherd of thy people: Grant that when we hear his voice we may know him who calleth us each by name, and follow where he doth lead; who, with thee and the Holy Spirit, liveth and reigneth, one God for ever and ever. Amen." Sing "Savior, like a Shepherd Lead Us."

Fourth Sunday after Easter: The theme for this Sunday is Christ, the sure Foundation. This is reflected in John 14:6 where Jesus says to Thomas, "I am the way, the truth and the life: no man cometh unto the Father, but by me." Ps. 66 is a wonderful hymn of adoration. As you pray it keep in mind that all the blessings outlined here are available to us because of Christ. Sing the hymn "Christ Is Made the Sure Foundation."

Fifth Sunday after Easter: The collect for today begins, "O God, who hast prepared for those who love thee such good things as pass man's understanding." In keeping with this attitude of gratitude, focus on praise and thanksgiving, especially for the beautiful world God has made, and pray Ps. 148. Notice the orderly structure of the psalm, proceeding from the heavens where God is worshiped by the angelic hosts, to earth where all are included in the call "praise ye the Lord." Sing "For the Beauty of the Earth." Count the blessings named.

Sixth Sunday after Easter: This, the last Sunday of the Easter season looks both forward and backward as it is the Sunday after Ascension Day and the Sunday before Pentecost (or Whitsunday). The collect from the *Book of Common Prayer* reflects this looking-both-directions aspect of the day: "O God, the King of glory, who hast exalted thine only Son Jesus Christ with great triumph unto thy kingdom in heaven; We beseech thee, leave us not comfortless, but send to us thine Holy Ghost to comfort us, and exalt us unto the same place whither our Savior Christ is gone before." Appropriately Ps. 47 praises God who is "The King of All." Conclude your prayer time with singing "Praise, My Soul, the King of Heaven."

PART III

Praying

the Collect
for Purity
for Pentecost

The Collect for Purity

Almighty God, unto whom all hearts are open, all desires known, and from whom no secrets are hid: Cleanse the thoughts of our hearts by the inspiration of thy Holy Spirit, that we may perfectly love thee, and worthily magnify thy holy Name; through Christ our Lord. Amen.

13

Waiting for Inspiration and Power: Pentecost Sunday

It was an almost bare room: a few wooden benches and stools, a table in the center with a basket of bread and cheese on it. Several men and women sat in various postures—some of resigned waiting, others of impatience. James, always the man of action, paced restlessly. "Do you realize we've been waiting here for more than a week? I mean, think of all the work we could have gotten done in that time!"

John answered in his quiet voice. "Yes, James, we're all well aware of that. But the Lord told us to wait. He said something like—"

"—I remember exactly," Andrew interrupted. "He said, 'Do not leave Jerusalem, but wait for the gift my Father promised. John baptized with water, but in a few days you will be baptized with the Holy Spirit.'"

James turned sharply. "Yeah, yeah. I know. I was there too. But He also said we were to go into all the world and carry the gospel to every creature. Seems to me we should be about it instead of sitting around here eating cheese."

John patted the cushion next to him as if to encourage James to settle down. "But isn't that what we're waiting for—the power to carry out His commission? Remember, He said, 'You shall receive power when the Holy Spirit has come upon you; and you shall be my witnesses—'"

"I know, I know. But when?"

And 2,000 years later, isn't that what we're still asking? When will we see the power of the Spirit really fulfilled in our lives, in our world? When will God's plan be revealed? When will . . . ? In our own waiting we can draw strength from thinking of the disciples' waiting and the glorious fulfillment of the promise on the Day of Pentecost. And we can know that just as God was faithful to fulfill His promise to them, so will He be to us—if we wait.

As Robert Webber says, Pentecost is an end and a beginning. It was an end to the disciples' waiting and a beginning to their missionary work. In the church year it is the end of the Easter season. "It is the day when the church senses the all-pervasive power of Easter as the Spirit is unleashed on Creation"; and it is the beginning of a new day in the life of the church. For now, as 2,000 years ago, "as the church is empowered by the Spirit, the message of the risen Lord is trumpeted around the world."[1]

Pentecost was originally a Jewish festival, celebrated 50 days after Passover, just as we now celebrate Pentecost 50 days after Easter. (The word *Pentecost* means 50 days.) As the second most important feast day of the church (after Easter) Pentecost was also a traditional day for baptisms. In England the day became popularly known as Whitsunday, after the white robes worn by the baptismal candidates.

In *A Continual Feast,* a cookbook with recipes for all the Christian feasts (now there's a brilliant idea!) Evelyn Birge Vitz recounts the medieval practices of celebrating Pentecost. Churches were constructed with "Holy Ghost holes" in the ceiling. On Pentecost, to the sound of trumpets "down through the hole would be lowered a great disk often painted with golden rays, and with a white dove, symbol of the Holy Spirit, painted on it. In some places pigeons or doves would be released into the church through the hole. Elsewhere roses were dropped. A few churches tried dropping burning straw. Alas, unlike the flames described in Acts, this fire did not hover over the faithful but fell right on them; the practice was discontinued."[2]

Focusing on this Pentecostal power in a new way, John Wesley's preaching ushered in a great age of revivalism that could be said to correspond to the pattern of that first Pentecost. As Wesley proclaimed in his "Sermon on the Holy Spirit," which he preached on Whitsunday in Oxford in 1736, Pentecost brought the "Spirit which giveth life; a Spirit, not only promised, but actually conferred; which should both enable Christians now to live unto God, and fulfil precepts even more spiritual than the former; and restore them hereafter to perfect life, after the ruins of sin and death. The incarnation, preaching, and death of Jesus Christ were designed to represent, proclaim, and purchase for us this gift of the Spirit; and therefore says the Apostle, 'The Lord is that Spirit.'"[3]

So in that same Spirit today we can pray in the words of the *Book of Common Prayer:* "O God, who on this day didst teach the hearts of thy faithful people by sending to them the light of thy Holy Spirit: Grant us by the same Spirit to have a right judgment in all things, and evermore to rejoice in his holy comfort; through the merits of Christ Jesus our Savior, who liveth and reigneth with thee, in the unity of the same Spirit, one God, world without end. Amen."

PRAYING FOR PERFECT LOVE

This was to be the greatest day of his life. The cathedral of Old Sarum, which he had so long labored to complete, was to be consecrated today. This meant more to Osmund than any other of his illustrious accomplishments, including accompanying his uncle William when he came from Normandy to claim the throne of England in 1066, his service as William's chaplain and compiler of the Domesday Book, his installation as chancellor of England, or his ordination as bishop of Salisbury. This cathedral atop the ancient hill fort near the River Avon, which had been brought to glorious realization by the sheer force of his personal energy and determination, could now shine forth as a beacon of God's kingdom on earth. And Osmund was determined that his reforms in church law and in the liturgy would influence the form of worship in all of England.

But first, in this moment of quiet between his past accomplishments and the busyness of the day that was to be filled with all the liturgical pomp and mystical ceremony the age was capable of, in this one moment Osmund would have his space of quiet devotions. A few minutes alone with God before he went forth to do his best to share God with all the world. Osmund knelt at the prie-dieu where a stream of early morning sun fell through the solitary small window.

"Deus cui omne cor patet et omnis voluntas loquitur, et quem nullum latet secretum: purifica per infusionem sancti Spiritus cogitationes cordis nostri: ut perfecte te diligere et digne laudare mereamur. Per Christum," he prayed in words from the 7th-century *Leonine Sacramentary*. ("God to whom every heart and every inclination is spoken, and to whom no mystery is concealed; purify us by the infusion of the Holy Spirit counseling our hearts, make us perfect and grant that we may be worthy to love and praise you. Through Christ.")

Osmund concluded his private prayers, donned his vestments, and went forth to serve God. And the lovely, simple prayer, which he included in his Sarum missal, became one of the standard prayers for all the churches in England—as it still is today. It was Thomas Cranmer, first archbishop of Canterbury, however, who, when writing the first *English Prayer Book* in 1548, moved the prayer from use for the priests' private devotions to congregational use.

The central concepts contained in this prayer of the worshiper being cleansed wholly and then expressing that entire sanctification in worthy and majestic praise, were the golden themes that led to the great revivals that swept England and America in the 18th and 19th centuries. John Wesley declared this prayer to contain the very heart of his doctrine of holiness. He quoted it 10 times in his sermons and letters, prayed it regularly in his private devotions and public services, and made it the opening prayer after the Lord's Prayer in his Communion service. Christians today who desire personal heart purity should pray it no less regularly.

This collective prayer is highly reminiscent of a much older prayer for purity, Ps. 51: "Purge me with hyssop, and I shall be clean: wash me, and I shall be whiter than snow" (v. 7). "Create in me a clean heart, O God; and renew a right spirit within me" (v. 10). "And my tongue shall sing aloud of thy righteousness. O Lord, open my lips; and my mouth shall shew forth thy praise" (vv. 14-15).

Traditional prayers and worship forms of the church are full of petitions for that holiness without which, the Scripture everywhere declares, no man shall see the Lord. And these are all summed up in those comprehensive words: "Cleanse the thoughts of our hearts by the inspiration of thy Holy Spirit, that we may perfectly love thee, and worthily magnify thy holy name." Over and over again throughout the ages "cleanse us from all unrighteousness" has been the cry of the committed Christian's heart. We can do no better than to make it the cry of our hearts too.

Prayer Guide
Praying for Purity

1. Pray the Collect for Purity as it is written on page 84. Now write the prayer in your journal, personalizing it. An example might be: "Almighty God, my heart is open to You, You know all my desires . . ."

2. The Old Testament prophets foretold the coming of the Holy Spirit. Read Isa. 11:2-5; Ezek. 36:25-28; and Joel 2:28-29. What was the Holy Spirit to do through Jesus when Christ lived on earth?

What is the Holy Spirit to do in the world?

What will the Spirit do through us if we allow Him to?

3. What were some of Jesus' teachings about the Holy Spirit? Read John 3:5; 14:26; 15:26; 16:7-14.

4. Before the believers could receive the Holy Spirit they had to obey Christ's commandment to wait. Read Acts 1:4-5; Rom. 8:25; Gal. 5:5. How do you feel about waiting?

Why is it important?

5. Read or sing the Isaac Watts hymn "Come, Holy Spirit, Heavenly Dove." What are some of the things the hymn writer petitions the Holy Spirit to do?

6. How would our world be different if more people prayed, as in the Collect for Purity, to have their thoughts cleansed by the Holy Spirit and sought to love God perfectly and worship Him worthily?

7. How could regularly praying this prayer change your life?

8. Just as we festooned each petition of the Lord's Prayer with our own thoughts and desires, we can enhance and personalize this ancient prayer.

Festooning the Collect for Purity

What do I mean when I pray to

"Almighty God"? _____

_____

"All desires are known"

What are the desires of my heart? _____

_____

"From whom no secrets are hid"
What are my secrets? _____

_____

"Cleanse the thoughts of our hearts"
Do you have thoughts and desires that need to be cleansed? _____

_____

"The inspiration of thy Holy Spirit"
Have you opened your life completely to the leading of the Holy Spirit? If not, why? _____

_____

"Perfectly love you"
How would you like to show your love for God? _____

_____

"Worthily magnify your holy name"
What would you like to be empowered to do for Him? _____

_____

"Through Christ our Lord"
What does it mean to pray "through Christ" as your Lord? _____

_____

Now write your festooned collect in your prayer journal. Pray it every day this week.

14 Past, Present, Future: Trinity Sunday

My mother was a lady of great dignity, but she also had a wacky sense of humor. When she and my father moved to a retirement center, it seemed every week that she had a new joke about aging. One of her favorites was about the three old brothers who lived together: One day Mike went upstairs to take a bath. A few minutes later he called down, "Hey, Joe! I'm standing here with one foot in the water and one out. Am I getting into the tub or out of it?"

Joe shook his head. "The old fool." Then he hollered. "Stay where you are, I'll be right there." At the top of the stairs he stopped and looked around. A moment later he called down, "Hey, Bob! Am I going upstairs or down?"

Bob shook his head. "Those old fools. I'm thankful I'm not like them—knock on wood." A moment later he looked around. "Was that the front door or the back?"

Well, somehow that story makes me think of in-between times—those occasions that look backward and forward. Trinity Sunday is one of those times. We look back to Pentecost and the whole Easter season, which it culminates, and we look forward to Kingdomtide, which it ushers in.

The Sunday after Pentecost has been celebrated as the Feast of the Holy and Undivided Trinity from early times, when it was a special day for reinstating those accused of heresy. (Perhaps because the most common heresies had to do with the doctrine of the Trinity?) Anyway, Trinity Sunday has been an official feast day of the church since 1334. It marks the conclusion of the liturgical commemorations of the life of Christ and the descent of the Holy Spirit by a celebration embracing God in all three Persons.

Although the doctrine that the one God exists in three Persons and one substance, Father, Son, and Holy Spirit is considered the central belief of Christian theology, the word *Trinity* is not found in Scripture. It was first used in the second century by a Greek theologian.

It is important to understand, however, that we are not celebrating a doctrine. Rather, we celebrate the God whose revelation of himself is an interaction of love between Persons. The doctrine developed as Christians attempted to express in human terms the inexpressible—our experience of God. As we grope to understand our experience of the tri-une God and His actions toward us, we find ourselves children of the Father, while at the same time the brother or sister of God incarnate, and the dwelling place of His Spirit. This we celebrate.

"There are three that bear record in heaven, the Father, the Word, and the Holy Ghost: and these three are one." 1 John 5:7 was John Wes-ley's favorite scripture on the topic of the Trinity, and the scripture he used as his sermon text almost every Trinity Sunday. He said belief in the Trinity is one of the great fundamentals of the faith, but that it is not necessary to believe in any one explanation of it. "I know not that any well-judging man would attempt to explain them at all. One of the best tracts that that great man Dean Swift (best known to us for his *Gulliver's Travels*) ever wrote was his 'Sermon upon the Trinity.' Herein he shows, that 'all who endeavoured to explain it at all, have utterly lost their way; have, above all other persons, hurt the cause which they intended to promote.'"

With such authority it might be best to put behind us memories of even the most earnest of Vacation Bible School teachers demonstrating how three parts—white, yolk, and shell—make one egg; or even the charming stories of St. Patrick approaching the druid Maccu Michlu armed only with a vibrant green shamrock.

"I insist upon no explication at all," Wesley says. Rather he would "insist only on the direct words, unexplained, just as they lie in the text: "There are three that bear record in heaven, the Father, the Word, and the Holy Ghost: and these three are one."

And so, in this simple and profound faith we can pray the model prayer from *A Collection of Forms of Prayer, for Every Day in the Week:*

Almighty God, Father of all mercies, I, thy unworthy servant, desire to present myself, with all humility, before thee, to offer my morning sacrifice of love and thanksgiving.

Glory be to thee, O most adorable Father, who, after thou had finished the work of creation, entered into thy eternal rest.

Glory be to thee, O holy Jesus, who having through the eternal Spirit, offered thyself a full, perfect, and sufficient sacrifice for the sins of the whole world, rose again the third day from the dead, and had all power given thee both in heaven and on earth.

Glory be to thee, O blessed Spirit, who, proceeding from the Father and the Son, came down in fiery tongues on the Apostles on the first day of the week, and enabled them to preach the glad tid-ings of salvation to a sinful world, and have ever since been moving on the faces of men's souls, as thou did once on the face of the great deep, bringing them out of that dark chaos in which they were involved.

Glory be to thee, O holy, undivided Trinity, for jointly concurring in the great work of our redemption, and restoring us again to the glorious liberty of the sons of God. Glory be to thee, . . . Let thy Holy Spirit, who, on the first day of the week, descended in miraculous gifts on thy Apostles, descend on me.

PRAYING WITH OPTIMISM

My third grader came home from school in a deep, dark funk. "I hate school. I hate recess. I hate playing the piano. I hate . . ."

"Whoa. Now, look. I understand that you've had a bad day. But about an equal number of good and bad things happen every day. You just have to decide which you're going to pay most attention to. . . ." And I proceeded to help him look on the bright side by making a happiness list.

Pollyanna? No, basic theology. Yes, we live in a fallen world. Yes, we are all born with original sin. But there is something more original than original sin, and that's original righteousness. There is desperate evil and ugliness all around us; but there is also great beauty and goodness.

We are not to gloss over human depravity. We are called "to know ourselves as also we are known by Him to whom all hearts are open." We are to be deeply sensible of our own unworthiness, of the universal depravity of our nature. In contrast, however, to the despairing pessimism and mood of darkness that seems to permeate so much of Christian thought, the good news is that depravity is not total. I'm sure you've noticed my fondness for the ideas of John Wesley, and it is precisely because he saw the optimism in the divine plan. In his sermon "The Mystery of Iniquity" he says,

> It is certain that "God made man upright"; perfectly holy and perfectly happy: But by rebelling against God, man destroyed himself, lost the favour and the image of God, and entailed sin, with its attendant, pain, on himself and all his posterity. Yet his merciful Creator did not leave him in this helpless, hopeless state: He immediately appointed his Son, his well-beloved Son, "who is the brightness of his glory, the express image of his person," to be the Saviour of men; . . . who, by his almighty Spirit, should heal the sickness of their souls, and restore them not only to the favour, but to "the image of God wherein they were created."[1]

It was Wesley's particular vision that the image of God in man, defaced at the Fall, could be restored through complete heart cleansing, which he called sanctification. This is, he said,

> No other than love, the love of God and of all mankind; the loving God with all our heart and soul, and strength, as having first loved us,—as the fountain of all the good we have, and of all we

ever hope to enjoy; and the loving every soul which God hath made. This is the great medicine of life; the never-failing remedy for all the evils of a disordered world; for all the miseries and vices of men. Wherever this is, there are virtues and happiness going hand in hand; there is humbleness of mind, gentleness, long-suffering, the whole image of God. This religion of love, and joy, and peace, has its seat in the inmost soul; but is ever showing itself by its fruits, continually springing up . . . spreading virtue and happiness to all around it. . . .'

And the whole of it is beautifully summed up in that one comprehensive petition, "cleanse the thoughts of our hearts by the inspiration of thy Holy Spirit, that we may perfectly love thee, and worthily magnify thy holy name."[2]

I fear I'm sounding a bit like a stuck record. But the frequent—almost constant—repetition of these beautiful words is what is needed to make them become a vital part of the believer's thought pattern—part of the very rhythm of life—like breathing or heartbeat.

And since such complete cleansing can come only by the inspiration of the Holy Spirit, we can pray today with the 11th-century priests at their private devotions, with Anglican worshipers through more than 450 years, and with reformers and revivalists of the past, for the inspiration of the Holy Spirit, both in an instantaneous cleansing and in a continual growth in grace for the moment-by-moment sustenance that brings us closer to Him.

The results of this cleansing of our hearts and minds by the Holy Spirit are twofold, inward and outward: First, the inward: "that we may perfectly love thee." The classic definition of perfect love is Matt. 22:37: "Thou shalt love the Lord thy God with all thy heart, and with all thy soul, and with all thy mind." In his sermon "The Almost Christian" Wesley says, "Such a love is this, as engrosses the whole heart, as takes up all the affections, as fills the entire capacity of the soul, and employs the utmost extent of all its faculties.

"He that thus loves the Lord his God, his spirit continually 'rejoiceth in God his Saviour.' His delight is in the Lord, his Lord and his All, to whom 'in everything he giveth thanks. All his desire is unto God, and to the remembrance of his name.'"[3]

Praying for the Holy Spirit to cleanse our hearts so that we can love God perfectly is no casual matter. This is not for the dilettante or the dabbler. It is only for serious Christians who want to walk so close to God that their will is inseparable from God's will.

And so we work from the inward to the outward. From this perfect love we are to go out and worthily magnify His holy name. Worthily magnifying the name of God is itself a twofold process as we express our love to God and to our neighbor, as in the second part of the Great Commandment, "Thou shalt love thy neighbour as thyself" (Matt. 22:39b).

In past times, those who gave themseves fully to this great love became famous for their good works as they started schools for the destitute, started orphanages, visited the sick, fed the hungry, and ministered to prisoners, as only a few examples. Today we carry on this work when we participate in evangelism and missions programs, inner-city ministries, or compassionate ministries both at home and abroad.

And God must be worthily magnified in our worship as well. We must keep our worship holy as we worship a holy God. We must keep our minds and hearts focused on God the Father, Son, and Holy Spirit, and not on ourselves or on our needs or our emotions. I have found that praying a prayer so profound in doctrine and so rich in poetry as the Collect for Purity can enhance my spiritual growth and help my worship to be a worthy magnifying of His name.

Or, once again in the words of my favorite preacher:

Leaning on our Beloved, even Christ in us the hope of glory, who dwelleth in our hearts by faith, who likewise is ever interceding for us at the right hand of God, we receive help from him to think, and speak, and act, what is acceptable in his sight. Thus does he prevent [go before] them that believe, in all their doings and further them with his continual help; so that all their designs, conversations, and actions are "begun, continued, and ended in him." Thus doth he "cleanse the thoughts of their hearts, by the inspiration of his Holy Spirit, that they may perfectly love him, and worthily magnify his holy name."[4]

Prayer Guide
Praying for the Holy Spirit

1. Read Gen. 1:26; 18:1-3; Matt. 3:16-17; 28:19; 2 Cor. 13:14; 1 John 5:7. From earliest times Christian scholars have seen representations of the Trinity in these scriptures. Explain.

2. Members of the Holy Club in 18th-century Oxford University were to ask themselves every Sunday: "Have I used a Collect at nine, twelve and three, aloud at my own room: deliberately, seriously, fervently?" Have you prayed the collect in this spirit? If so, what were the results? If not, why?

3. Is it important for a Christian to be completely open to the work of the Holy Spirit in his or her life?

How do the first phrases of the collect lead the worshiper to this openness?

4. How can we perfectly love God? (see Rom. 5:5). How would such perfect love change my life?

5. What does it mean to magnify God's name worthily? How will this be reflected in our worship?

6. A collect is a short prayer with three parts: (1) an invocation, usually to God; (2) a petition; (3) a pleading of Christ's name or an ascription of glory to God. Following this form, write, in your prayer journal, a collect on any topic of concern to you.

7. Last week we prayed the Collect for Purity, inserting our own names. This week pray it for someone else, such as, "Almighty God, let Mary's heart be open to you. You know her desires. Cleanse her thoughts . . ."

8. Are there things you need to add to your festooned collect on page 88? Continue praying it daily this week.

PART IV

Praying

Without Ceasing
Through
Kingdomtide

Making the Ordinary Extraordinary: Kingdomtide or Ordinary Time

My daughter said to me, "Mother, why don't we have any flowers?" I was flabbergasted. "What do you mean—no flowers? We have red roses and pink roses and yellow roses and white roses. What else is there?"

"No. I mean regular flowers. Like pansies and snapdragons and daisies."

"Oh." Well, OK. She had a point. Those are flowers, too, I suppose. "OK. You want flowers, you plant them. There's plenty of dirt out there."

That was several years ago. Now our garden blossoms like a rose—and like so much more as well.

And here we are, at the end of spring, in the planting season. The time when we have to decide what we want to plant in our garden in order to reap the harvest of beauty or usefulness later in the year. Likewise, we must spend the next several months tending that garden and watching it grow. And, as I learned from my daughter's prompting, one-of-a-kind, elegant plants can be greatly enhanced by a background of the comfortable, less exotic.

And so it is in our worship and prayer life. We need the festivals. We need the great seasons of self-examination and contrition and times of celebration, but we also need the times of quiet growth. We now enter the season of the church year commonly called ordinary time—the time without festivals—when we get down to the day-to-day work of garden growing and Kingdom building.

The festive cycle, Advent through Pentecost, focuses on the life of Christ. The nonfestive season focuses on the life of the Church. The designation *ordinary time,* however, which came into use in the middle ages, was not meant to imply that the season was dull, but merely that the order of the service (the ordinary) did not vary from the regular schedule. In order to accentuate the positive and emphasize the Kingdom-building aspect of this season many Christians today have adopted the term *Kingdomtide.* This term was apparently coined in 1937 by an ecumenical council that published a book on the Christian year. The liturgical color for the season is green, which is particularly appropriate as it is a season to focus on growing in grace.

The concept of the kingdom of God, or kingdom of heaven, lies in the Old Testament where the kingship of God is acknowledged. This is beautifully expressed in Pss. 97 and 99 that both begin, "The Lord reigneth." God's reign was expected to bring with it order and justice, thereby manifesting God's purpose for creation.

Jesus began His ministry by proclaiming that "the kingdom of God is at hand" (Mark 1:15). This is a kingdom both present and yet to come. In order to prepare for the future Kingdom we must cultivate our roles in the here and now. And the place to start is with our prayer life. Like a garden where a few special plants are set off and nurtured by an underpinning of sturdy perennials, so the specially festooned prayers we focus on will flourish in a prayer life bedded in constant, open communion with our Lord.

PRAYING LIKE BREATHING

Twenty years ago when we moved to our home in the Boise foothills we were informed by our contractor, who framed our basement himself after his crew walked off because of the danger, that our sandy soil was "just like tiny marbles." We had no idea what that would mean in terms of gardening. But we learned. For years my husband said that somewhere in China there was a garden burgeoning with incredible lushness because all our fertilizer was draining straight down to it. Then I got on to composting. We now have a thriving garden to match that one in China. Through years of careful building up of the soil we've provided an environment in which our plants can grow. Likewise, by learning to pray without ceasing we can build a climate that will provide a nourishing base for all of our spiritual life.

Just as there are two aspects to gardening—the active seasons of planting and harvest, and the quiet times of waiting patiently for growth; so there are two kinds of prayer—active and passive. We have spent our study so far on active, external prayer. Now it's time to turn our attention to the passive, internal, constant prayer that is the living in the presence of God to which the apostle Paul refers as praying without ceasing.

Praying without ceasing is, very simply, constantly living in the awareness of and in yieldedness to God's presence. It is an openness to God that unblocks grace to us and to the world and helps make the petition for His will to be done "on earth as it is in heaven" a reality. Prayer is our openness to God. His hearing is God's openness to us. Praying without ceasing is living in this open channel. It is unblocking our resistance to grace.

The commandment of God that we are to pray without ceasing is founded on our urgent need for His grace to preserve the life of God in the soul. This spiritual life can no more subsist one moment without His grace than the body can without air. I love Wesley's all-encompassing definition of praying without ceasing: "Whether we think of or speak to God, whether we act or suffer for God, all is prayer when we have no other object than God's love, and the desire of pleasing God. All that a Christian does, even in eating and sleeping, is prayer, when it is done in simplicity, according to the order of God, without either adding to or diminishing from it by one's own choice."[1] Living in an awareness of His presence means we can make God's presence the groundedness of everything else in our lives, so that God becomes the resting place of our thoughts just as truly as a richly fertilized seedbed is the whole basis of successful gardening.

Catherine of Siena says, "We cannot truly possess God except by giving ourselves to Him with an undivided love. And without prayer we cannot arrive at that state in which the whole heart is given to God without taking anything back."[2] And then the English writer Gregory Dix goes on, "It is only by constant intercourse with God that we learn what is that fullness of God with which we are to be filled. . . . It is in prayer that the image of God in us is most brightly burnished and most splendidly displayed in this world and in eternal life. Prayer is an abiding state."[3]

Dix talks about, "'The spirit of prayer,' a dim but unfailing awareness of the fact of God somewhere at the back of the mind," and says that this "ought to be the aim of every Christian who takes his religion seriously. . . . Yet for the most part, such prayer will be simply a return to the bare fact of God. It is not so much a matter of thinking about God as of thinking of Him. It is living in a spirit of perpetual reverence."[4]

I began my journey with this type of prayer many years ago when I discovered a tiny blue paperback book. I was so excited I couldn't wait to tell the next class I taught: "I've found this wonderful book; it's revolutionized my prayer life; it's called *The Practice of the Presence of God*!" I waved the book in front of them, and they sat there calmly nodding their heads. And I said, "Oh. Am I the last person in the world to discover this?" One young woman on the front row, bless her, had the grace to shake her head. Maybe she was just being tactful, but I did feel better.

In case anyone else out there is a late bloomer like I was, this tiny book recounts the experience of a 17th-century lay brother who wanted to join a monastery so he could spend all his time in peace and quiet meditating and praying. And, guess what, he found himself assigned to run the kitchen! You can see why, as a mother of four young children, I instantly identified with this man. Brother Lawrence had to get up early in the morning and go to the busy market and haggle with merchants for produce and then go home and cook it and serve it and then wash the pots and then start the next meal—well, we've all been there, right? But Brother Lawrence discovered that God was with him in the market-place and in the serving hall and standing over the cook pots and sink every bit as much as in the chapel or in his cell, and that, as he says, "We can always see God and His glory in everything we do, say, and un-dertake; and the end we should seek is to be the most perfect adorers of God in this life."[5]

But lest you think this only works for 17th-century monks, let me share with you from the introduction to the 1977 edition of Brother Lawrence's book by 20th-century writer Henri Nouwen: "Our lives are fragmented. There are so many things to do, so many events to worry about, so many people to think of, so many experiences to work through, tasks to fulfill, demands to respond to, needs to pay attention to. Often it seems that just keeping things together asks for enormous energy."[6] Unfortunately, I can't think of a more accurate description of life at the turn of the millennium.

Nouwen's solution to this is "not saying prayers but a way of living in which all we do becomes prayer. A prayerful life is a life in which all we do is done to the glory of God and God alone."[7]

Brother Lawrence said that his principal concern during his more than 40 years in religion was to be with God always—to do nothing, to say nothing, and to think nothing that would displease Him. Whenever he felt he had strayed a bit from that divine presence, God would make himself felt in his soul to recall it to Him. And Brother Lawrence would respond with a few simple words such as, "My God, here I am, all Yours; Lord make me according to Your heart."[8]

Brother Lawrence, as other writers have done, calls this "making way for grace." He says those who have been breathed on by the Holy Spirit move forward even while sleeping, but to achieve this the heart must be emptied of all other things, for God wishes to possess it entire-ly. "A little lifting up of the heart suffices; a little remembrance of God, . . . even though made on the march and with sword in hand, are prayers which, short though they may be, are nevertheless very pleasing to God. We need to repeat often during the day these little acts of interior ado-ration."[9]

Thomas Merton says this is "not so much a way to find God as a way of resting in him whom we have found."

One ancient form of such praying without ceasing is the "Jesus prayer" practiced for centuries by monks of the Orthodox church. They sought to abandon all distracting thoughts and to pray without ceasing using the phrase "Lord Jesus, be merciful to me a sinner" as a rhythm of breathing. I don't particularly recommend this as a model—but the point is the practice of keeping the name of Jesus ever present in the ground of one's being and, as Merton says, living in a climate of "aware-ness, gratitude, and a totally obedient love that seeks nothing but to please God."

A teacher who deals with these ancient concepts in a modern appli-cation is Ron DelBene in his book *The Breath of Life.* He says, "We are challenged to become prayer, to be so God-centered that we become other-centered and think of prayer as a gift of ourselves to another per-son."[10]

DelBene goes on to teach a step-by-step process for incorporating this form of prayer in one's daily life, but it is the underlying concepts and principles of such a life of constant prayer that I want to emphasize here. Julian of Norwich, a 14th-century English mystic, and a particular favorite of mine, expresses the true heart of the matter, "The fruit and the purpose of prayer is to be oned with and like God in all things." The concept of "Oneing" is Dame Julian's unique expression of a life lived in perfect harmony with God.

And the early 20th century English mystic Evelyn Underhill agrees, "This is not mere pious fluff. This is a terribly practical job. It is the only way in which we can contribute to the bringing in of the kingdom of God. Humanitarian politics will not do it. Theological restatement will not do it. Holiness will do it."[11]

And finally, from that classic of contemplative prayer *The Cloud of Un-knowing,* "Nourish in your heart the lively longing for God. Though this loving desire is certainly God's gift, it is up to you to nurture it. . . . Press on then. Our Lord is always ready. He awaits only your co-operation."[12]

Prayer Guide
Living in the Kingdom of Prayer

1. Whereas each of the festive seasons has a distinct theme such as the birth of Christ, His death and resurrection, or the coming of the Holy Spirit, themes for ordinary time are drawn from studying various sections of Scripture, usually the Gospels. Think about your own life. What topic of Bible study would be most applicable to your life for the next six months until we begin the sea-son of Advent?

With the help of a concordance or the advice of a teacher or pastor, list the scriptures you want to study during this time.

What specific goals do you hope to reach through this study?

Record your progress in your journal.

2. There is no richer teaching on the kingdom of heaven than in the Gospel of Matthew. Read Matt. 13:24-52. List the seven different images Jesus uses to teach about the kingdom of heaven. Which one is the most meaningful to you? Why?

3. Read Matt. 18:23-35. This is the story of the unforgiving servant. Look back over your festooning and the prayers you wrote concerning "forgive us our trespasses as we forgive those who trespass against us." Record your thoughts.

4. Read Matt. 20:1-16. No matter what my goal, I so often feel that I've

started too late and accomplished too little. If you're like that, too, what comfort can we find in this story Jesus told?

5. Read the parable of the wise and foolish virgins, Matt. 25:1-13. Ask the Lord what you need to do to have your lamp trimmed, your loins girt, and yourself in actual readiness to attend the Bridegroom. Record His answer.

6. Read Matt. 25:14-30. I am a two-talent person. Sometimes I long to have been a five-talent person, but this parable is of great comfort to me because its emphasis is not on the ability we possess but rather on our fidelity in improving what we have. And then there are the times I have felt as if the Lord said, "Donna, you've been faithful over a few things, now you can work even harder." And so I keep trying. What abilities, jobs, challenges has the Lord given you that you need to be improving for your own soul's sake and to build the Kingdom?

How do you plan to set about this work?

Record your progress in your journal throughout the period of ordinary time.

7. Christ told all these parables to teach us about His kingdom. After studying them, describe some aspects of the nature of the Kingdom.

8. The first step in learning to pray without ceasing and to living in the Kingdom with the channel of grace always unblocked is to obey Rom. 12:1. Write the verse here.

How can we do this in our prayer life? in relation to others? in taking Communion?

9. Ron DelBene and many others who teach methods of praying without ceasing instruct the student to form a short (three- or four-word) prayer that reflects the deepest cry of your heart and repeat it over and over silently with the rhythm of your breathing. Concentrate on your breath prayer at quiet moments until you find yourself praying it without conscious volition. Write your prayer.

Pray this way for several weeks. Record the experience in your prayer journal.

16 Seeking First the Kingdom of God

In the whole history of literature few works have touched more people than John Bunyan's *Pilgrim's Progress*. And no scene is more powerful than that at the end of Christian's journey when he enters into the kingdom of heaven. Kingdomtide is about living in the Kingdom now so that we, like Christian, will be able to enter into that true Kingdom of which this is but a shadow. Let me share Bunyan's vision with you:

Now, while they were thus drawing towards the gate, behold, a company of the heavenly host came out to meet them; to whom it was said by the other two Shining Ones, "These are the men that have loved our Lord when in the world, and that have left all for His holy name; and He hath sent us to fetch them, and we have brought them thus far on their desired journey, that they may go in and look their Redeemer in the face with joy."

Then the heavenly host gave a great shout, saying, "Blessed are they which are called to the marriage supper of the Lamb." There came out also at this time to meet them several of the King's trumpeters, clothed in white and shining raiment, who, with melodious noises and loud, made even the heavens to echo with their sound. These trumpeters saluted Christian and his fellow with ten thousand welcomes from the world.

These two men went in at the gate; and lo! as they entered, they were transfigured; and they had raiment put on that shone like gold. There were also that met them with harps and crowns, and gave them to them—the harps to praise withal, and the crowns in token of honor.

Then I heard in my dream that all the bells in the City rang again for joy, and that it was said unto them; "Enter ye into the joy of your Lord." I also heard the men themselves; that they sang with a loud voice, saying, "Blessing, and honor, and glory, and power be unto Him that sitteth upon the throne, and unto the Lamb, forever and ever!"[1]

This Kingdomtide we want to learn more about the Kingdom so we can live in it more fully now as we prepare for the future. As Christians we have been called from the vanities of the world, and from a religion of mere form, to the "pearl of great price," that "kingdom of God [which] is not meat and drink; but righteousness, and peace, and joy in the Holy Ghost" (Rom. 14:17).

As members of Christ and children of God we are joint partakers now of the present kingdom of God and fellow heirs of His eternal kingdom. We are to seek first this kingdom of God in our hearts; this righteousness, which is the gift and work of God, the image of God renewed in our souls; and, the promise is, all these other things will be added unto us. In seeking the peace and love of God we will find this Kingdom that cannot be moved.

The kingdom of God is that "peace of God, which passeth all understanding." Even now as His kingdom exists in a fallen world it is full of unspeakable glory. I often gaze in awe at the beauty of this world and find it impossible to imagine how much better a perfect world will be. The beauty we have around us now is a reflection of His beauty and His love shed abroad in our hearts by the Holy Spirit. This is that kingdom of heaven which is within us: "righteousness, and peace, and joy in the Holy Ghost." John Wesley defined *righteousness* as the life of God in the soul; the mind that was in Christ Jesus; the image of God stamped upon the heart, now renewed after the likeness of Him that created it. It is the love of God, because He first loved us, and it is the love of all humankind for His sake.

When one prays "Thy kingdom come" this Kingdom comes to a person as he or she repents and believes the gospel; and as he or she learns more of God and of His Son so is the kingdom of God begun here below, set up in the believer's heart.

The commandment to "Seek ye first the kingdom of God" gets to the very heart of a life of holiness. In order to do this we must be like Bunyan's Christian who, whether in the dungeons of the Castle of Despair, the distractions of Vanity Fair, the terrors of the Valley of the Shadow of Death, or the sweetness of Beulah Land, always pressed on toward the mark. One must allow Christ to reign in the heart and to dwell and rule in the heart and mind. Our goal must be perfect obedience to Christ. God must have sole dominion over us. He alone must reign without a rival. Wesley told his followers, "Let him possess all your heart, and rule alone. Let him be your one desire, your joy, your love; so that all that is within you may continually cry out, 'The Lord God omnipotent reigneth.'

"Except a man be thus born again, he cannot see the kingdom of God. But all who are thus born of the Spirit have the kingdom of God within them. Christ sets up his kingdom in their hearts—His kingdom of righteousness, peace, and joy in the Holy Ghost."[2] Central to living in this Kingdom is praying without ceasing. And one of the best ways of praying without ceasing is learning to pray without words—living so completely yielded to God through prayer that we are, in Julian of Norwich's term, "oned" with Him. One of the best methods for developing this prayer attitude is centering prayer.

Praying Without Words

Well, that's the way life is, isn't it? Just the time you think you've got it together, everything flies off in a dozen different directions.

I had been practicing centering prayer for several months when my mother became so ill I had to begin feeding her—so there went that special, set-aside 20 minutes every morning and evening. Then after she died I was really too exhausted. And then I was getting my daughter off to college. And then . . . And then a whole year had passed and my life was anything but centered. Things I had never dreamed could go wrong had gone wrong. It was time to make time for that prayer retreat I'd been talking about taking for the past three years.

"Just let everything go. Let the rhythms of the day quiet your spirit," my spiritual director said. Easy enough on that quiet green hillside covered with wildflowers overlooking an incredibly lush prairie dotted here and there with sheltered farmhouses. Prayer and Bible readings three times a day with the community—which I wanted to take at about twice the speed of my already-slowed-down companions—then quiet hours of reflection, prayer, and reading.

It sounds so easy. Why was I having such a hard time with it? Getting and keeping our lives centered in Jesus Christ is the hardest thing in the world—because it's the simplest. So let's try taking this step together—because I need all the help I can get.

Many of the spiritual stalwarts of the past spoke of praying without words. "I do not advise much talking in prayer, concentrate on keeping your mind in the presence of the Lord,"[3] Brother Lawrence said.

However, the ever-practical C. S. Lewis confessed, "For many years after my conversion I tried to pray without words at all—not to verbalise the mental acts. Even in praying for others I believe I tended to avoid their names and substituted mental images of them. I still think the prayer without words is the best—if one can really achieve it. But I now see that in trying to make it my daily bread I was counting on a greater mental and spiritual strength than I really have. To pray successfully without words one needs to be 'at the top of one's form.' Otherwise, the mental acts become merely imaginative or emotional acts—and a fabricated emotion is a miserable affair."[4]

Lewis concludes that even though reaching this ideal might be unrealistic most of the time, "For me words are in any case secondary. They are only an anchor—they are the movements of a conductor's baton: not the music."[5]

The 17th-century French mystic Francis de Sales says in his book *Introduction to the Devout Life,* placing yourself in the presence of God "consists of a lively, attentive realization of God's absolute presence, that is, that God is in all things and all places. There is no place or thing in this world where he is not truly present. Just as wherever birds fly they always encounter the air, so also wherever we go or wherever we are we find God present."[6] We know that intellectually, but intentionally cultivating an awareness of the fact, or as Francis de Sales says bringing it home to ourselves, is the heart of praying without ceasing, or as Thomas Keating puts it, "God is present to everything, yet we may not be present to God."[7]

Now, we really have two things going here. One is living in a constant state of an awareness of God's presence, and the other is a practice of entering into specific times of contemplative prayer, coming in complete openness to God and sitting before Him in companionable silence. One form of this more specific act is called centering prayer.

A person who seems to have achieved this perfection in her prayer life was Mother Teresa. In an interview on national television she was asked, "What do you say when you pray?"

Her answer, "I don't say anything, I listen."

Question, "What does God say?"

Answer, "God listens too."

This is centering prayer: Sitting in silence with God, open to Him. Yielded. Experiencing God. Feeling His heart. What does God's heart feel? Love. Pain. "Go, and do thou likewise."

Basically, centering prayer is learning to rest quietly in the presence of God at specific times during the day. Thomas Keating, the leader of the current centering prayer movement, says, "It is the opening of mind and heart—our whole being—to God beyond thoughts, words, and emotions. Moved by God's sustaining grace, we open our awareness to God, who we know by faith is within us, closer than breathing, closer than thinking, closer than choosing—closer than consciousness itself. Contemplative prayer is a process of interior transformation, a relationship initiated by God and leading, if we consent, to divine union."[8] And this can be achieved only through silence.

Silence. Aye, there's the rub—achieving silence in an age that denigrates quiet as "dead time." Gaymon Bennett, whom I value for his friendship and his poetry, wrote:

THE NOISE IS TOO MUCH WITH US

The noise is too much with us, night and noon;
The trees have stopped their woody ears and fled.
Little we know that's silent that's not dead.
We have given our peace away—a wasteful boon.
Those nights we heard stars singing to the moon
And afternoons when bees hummed to the flowers

And evenings when a laugh echoed for hours
Are gone forever with the tree frogs' tune.
We've bartered all that makes life worth the task
Of daily living for the price of oil,
Our farms and fields for an asphalt track,
And contemplations for a life of toil.
Will it be quiet in the tomb, I ask;
Or noises only muffled by the soil.

Yes, noise is the problem. But what do we do? How can we find the drowned-out silence within ourselves? Just telling people to be quiet will only make the problem worse. I found as an English teacher that there was nothing more frustrating for my students than simply saying, "Write a short story." But if I told them, "Look, there are rules to this game, there is a procedure to follow and a structure to be learned," then they would relax and their creative juices could flow. So it is even with something as personal and individual as sitting in silence with God.

Begin by choosing your sacred word, the word you will use as the centering focus of your prayer. The anonymous author of *The Cloud of Unknowing* says, "If you want to gather all your desire into one simple word that the mind can easily retain, choose a short word rather than a long one. A one-syllable word such as 'God' or 'love' is best. But choose one that is meaningful to you. Then fix it in your mind so that it will remain there come what may."[9]

Next choose a time and place where you can sit in uninterrupted comfort for about 20 minutes. Choose a place without distractions—not even sacred music or candles. I find that the first thing—the very first thing—in the morning is a good time. Second best for me is that late afternoon shifting-of-the-gears moment when I've quit work but don't have to start dinner yet. Late at night is not good. Oddly, rather than putting me to sleep as you might guess, I find centering prayer invigorating and have trouble getting to sleep if I practice it just before going to bed. On the other hand, if you do find yourself falling asleep during your prayer times it simply means you're exhausted. Allow yourself the renewal of sleep. Then pray when you're refreshed. Spiritual work doesn't look like much, but it's really the hardest work in the world. As C. S. Lewis says, "You have to be at the top of your form."

The standard teaching is to practice centering prayer twice a day for 20 minutes at a time. If the mere thought of that leaves you gasping, don't abandon hope. Simply do what you can; 2 or 3 minutes of quiet alone with God are better than no minutes alone with God.

"Yes, yes," I can hear you saying, "but what do we *do*?" Are you ready for this? You don't do anything. Sit quietly, comfortably, with your eyes closed and just *be*.

"But what about all the chatter in my mind? I can't keep thoughts out." Of course you can't. Thomas Keating suggests using the image of your mind as a stream. Let the thoughts pass through, flowing as boats on the stream. But don't you get on the boat. If you find yourself going down the stream with one of your thoughts, use your sacred word to get you back sitting quietly on the shore. Don't chant the word, simply use it to keep you centered and on the shore.

"But isn't this selfish? I could use the same amount of time to pray for my family and missionaries and all the suffering people in the world and . . ." Ah, yes. That was my first reaction when I began studying centering prayer. If you hadn't already guessed from reading previous chapters, I'm a laundry list pray-er—compulsive about it—forever dinging the ear of the Almighty about all the wonderful things I want Him to do. I mean—there are souls to be saved! this world needs revival!

Well, yes, that's certainly true. But one of the important things to understand is that contemplative prayer is an addition to your prayer life, not a substitute for anything else you've been doing. Continue your regular prayer and Bible reading just as always. Let this special time alone with God be your special treat—the little devotional bouquet you carry to savor in your heart. And as to the niggling idea at the back of your mind that you really could be going over your list again, listen once more to The Cloud of Unknowing, "One loving blind desire for God alone is more valuable in itself, more pleasing to God . . . more beneficial to your own growth, and more helpful to your friends . . . than anything else you could do."[10]

So when all the doubts arise and as you ask yourself, "What do you think you're doing? What do you want?" Answer with The Cloud of Unknowing, "God alone I seek and desire, only him." And that truly gets to the heart of the matter, because in this type of praying intentionality is everything. What do you intend when you come to God, when you dedicate these moments of your day to Him, when you sit alone with Him? It's important that you understand that you've not come to seek favors or to beg forgiveness or to do any other kind of spiritual work. You have come to be with Him.

The heart of holiness is being open to God. This is one very good way to open yourself to Him—as others have said, to open the channels so that grace can flow to you, and then, later, from you to other people. You can be a channel of grace to your world—but only if the channels between you and God are completely unblocked. Busyness and worry are two of the worst blockers. So start with not letting worry over whether or not you're doing your centering prayer "right" be a hindrance. The teacher who introduced me to this spiritual discipline said, "Remember, if you're sitting there, you're doing it right." And sitting there is the hardest part.

But there's no way to start except to start.

Prayer Guide
God and Me Alone

1. Centering prayer is one of the most powerful tools available to us for entering into the kingdom of God. Before we move ahead with the prayer, read Lev. 20:26, Luke 17:21, Mark 10:13-16, and Rom. 14:17. Spend some time meditating on the meaning of the Kingdom as a present reality. Record your thoughts.

2. A division exists in Christian thought as to which is more important— the Great Commission or the Great Commandment. Read and record Matt. 28:19. Read and record Matt. 22:36-38. Of course, both are important. But which do you believe is more foundational? Why?

3. How have I kept the first commandment? In what ways have I failed?

4. What are your greatest hindrances to spending time sitting quietly at Jesus' feet?

5. Are you willing to attempt setting these hindrances aside for 20 minutes twice a day? If so, ask the Lord to help you. If not, why?

6. Brainstorm your choice of a sacred word. Think of concepts or objects that are important to you, such as home, family, love.

Think of qualities of God for which you praise Him, such as holiness, goodness, beauty, grace.

Think of names of God such as *Lord, Jesus, Christ.*

Think of symbols of faith such as dove, cross, flame, spirit, cloud.

Think of praise words such as *glory, alleluia, hosanna.*

A word of one or two syllables is best, but it's most important that the word have special meaning for you. When you have chosen your word, write it down.

7. Record your intention as to time and place that you will sit in quiet with God. And what is your intention for this time?

8. At your chosen time sit quietly, comfortably. Open yourself to God. When thoughts enter your mind, say your sacred word and return to inner quietness. After 20 minutes close with saying the Lord's Prayer or simply go about the rest of your day. Record thoughts about your experience. Remember, don't judge it, just observe it.

9. Continue with this practice for several weeks. Write about the experience occasionally in your prayer journal.

10. Now that you have experienced both the more active form of praying without ceasing and the entirely passive centering prayer, decide which suits you best and continue practicing it throughout Kingdomtide—perhaps for the rest of your life.

Created in the Image of God

So here we were—brand-new grandparents dying to see that wonderful, tiny new being—surely the best God ever made! And there they were—our son Stanley and his wife, Kelly, with the precious new Thomas Fletcher Crow in Seoul, Korea! It seemed like forever from the first phone call until the pictures arrived—by the wonders of electronic media—on our computer screen. Within hours my husband had printed them off and was showing them to our friends—complete with a list of acceptable comments: "Obviously brilliant!" "Incredibly handsome!" "Just like his grandfather!"

Our closest friend took one look at the pictures, one look at my husband, and said, "Well, I don't know—I've never met Kelly's father."

Isn't it interesting how we always examine babies to determine who they resemble. And rightly so—heritage is important. We're delighted to see our good qualities passed on to our children—and the bad ones always come from the other side of the family. But even more, we should examine ourselves to see how well we resemble our Heavenly Father.

The fact that God created humanity in His own image is strongly stressed in the creation story: "And God said, Let us make man in our image, after our likeness. . . . So God created man in his own image, in the image of God created he him; male and female created he them" (Gen. 1:26-27). "In the image of God made he man" (9:6). But after that glorious beginning something happened. Every other reference to *image* in the Old Testament is related to graven image, carved image, molten image, golden image, image of Baal. And it's picked up again in the New Testament in Revelation with numerous references to the image of the beast.

What happened? Sin happened. The Fall happened. The image of God in man was damaged. Not erased, not hopelessly demolished, but seriously defaced. The original righteousness in which God created the world still existed—Satan was not powerful enough to do away with the goodness and beauty God built into His creation, but sin's scarring runs deep. So deep that God the Son had to return to earth, die on the Cross, and defeat Satan by rising to life again in order to make possible the restoration of the image of God in humankind in this life.

And it isn't until after the work of Christ was completed that we again find references in Scripture to humanity bearing the likeness of God: "he is the image and glory of God" (1 Cor. 11:7). "And as we have borne the image of the earthy, we shall also bear the image of the heavenly" (15:49). "But we all, with open face beholding as in a glass the glory of the Lord, are changed into the same image from glory to glory, even as by the Spirit of the Lord" (2 Cor. 3:18). "Who is the image of the invisible God, the firstborn of every creature" (Col. 1:15). "And have put on the new man, which is renewed in knowledge after the image of him that created him" (3:10).

This glorious restoration, however, isn't automatic. We are fallen creatures living in a fallen world. The work of Christ must be complete in our hearts and lives in order to lift us from this fallenness. First, of course, by going to Him in sorrow for our sins, confessing them, and seeking His forgiveness. Then by turning control of our lives over to Him completely, giving Him perfect freedom to complete that good work in us as we live fully in His light and beauty, growing closer and closer and more and more like Him every day.

If we are to have the image of God restored in us, we must "seek first the kingdom of God and His righteousness." We can do this only by spending more time with Him so that we can reflect His image. It can only be by knowing more about Him so our minds can follow His precepts. It can only be by letting His countenance shine upon us so that we can flower in the sun of His radiant glory and then open fully to Him.

A uniquely fragile wildflower called prairie smoke grows on Idaho's camas prairie. Each stalk begins with three reddish, star-shaped buds growing on slender stems with their faces bowed over looking steadily at the ground. But slowly a strange thing occurs. As the stalk pushes higher, one of the buds begins looking upward to the sun. And it's always the middle bud—the one that is the most centered. Then the miracle happens: after a few days of gazing at the sun the bud bursts into full flower—a ball of delicate silver strands that catch the morning dew and golden sunshine.

This way of holiness that enables our lives to blossom like the rarest of flowers is an inward thing—the life of God in our souls. Through this inward life we can actually participate in the divine nature, come to know the mind that was in Christ, and have our hearts renewed after the image of Him that created us. It sounds awesome, radical, even scary. But in fact, the only thing we should fear is falling short of the full image of God, of being less than our Creator intended us to be.

What is this image like? It will be different for each one of us, because God's intention for each of us is different. But to get an idea of what we're talking about, turn back to your festooned Lord's Prayer that we did in chapter 1. Examine the qualities of God you listed. As we are restored more and more to His image, we will reflect more and more of

His qualities. For example: God made man to be "holy as He that created him is holy; merciful as the Author of all is merciful; perfect as his Father in heaven is perfect. As God is love, so man, dwelling in love, dwelt in God, and God in him. God made him to be an image of his own eternity, an incorruptible picture of the God of glory. He was accordingly pure, as God is pure, from every spot of sin. He knew not evil in any kind or degree, but was inwardly and outwardly sinless and undefiled. He 'loved the Lord his God with all his heart, and with all his mind, and soul, and strength.'"[1] That's Wesley's description of the image of God: Holy, merciful, perfect, loving, incorruptible, pure—that's the image God wants to restore in us.

We are to stand fast in love, in the image of God wherein we are made. We are to love the Lord our God with all our heart. Desire nothing but God. Aim at God in every thought, in every word and work; and let all that is in us praise His holy name. There can be no higher calling. As a matter of fact, it is so high we have no hope of accomplishing it. Our only hope is to let Him accomplish it in us.

All of this is another way of saying as the apostle Paul did, "Whether therefore [we] eat, or drink, or whatsoever [we] do, [we are to] do all to the glory of God" (1 Cor. 10:31). And yet, this life of holiness is not a matter of outward things, such as eating and drinking, or even a matter of doing good or of church attendance. The life of God in the soul is a renewal of our mind in every desire and thought to reflect the One that created it. Through this life of God in our soul we can actually participate in the divine nature.

This complete turning from the old nature of fallen man toward the image of God can be accomplished in a moment. It is a matter of desiring with all our heart, mind, and strength to be like Him, to have nothing in our lives that is not of Him. The decision may take years to come to, but it can be made in an instant. The completeness of the image, however, will not be instantaneous—and aren't we glad! Wouldn't it be awful to have no place to go, no hope of improvement. To have to look at our lives and say, "Well, here I am. That's it, and there's nothing more to be done about it." I love the idea that though I may not be improving on the outside I can keep getting better and better on the inside. The more and more our minds are renewed in the image of Him that created us, we are more and more capable of His influences. As we live in daily communication with Him, we are more and more transformed into His likeness.

And so this matter of holiness is not a thing of fasting or asceticism or any bodily austerity, but rather of entering into the mind that was in Christ—a renewal of our soul in the image of God. One way to enter into this life of holiness is through praying the scriptures—the practice named Lectio Divina by sixth-century monks, but equally applicable to our lives today.

PRAYING THE SCRIPTURES

During Holy Week we experienced praying and chanting the Psalms and in the first weeks of Kingdomtide we focused on topical Bible study, but now we undertake a whole new approach to Bible reading. If you've been raised on the "three chapters a day and five on Sunday" method of reading your Bible through in a year, this contemplative method can revolutionize your Bible reading. And if you've been told—as I have—that serious, topical, expository Bible study is the only way to grow spiritually; and yet you find yourself bogging down—as I do—no matter how determined you are, here's a refreshing, guilt-free way of approaching God's Word.

The central understanding is that the Word of God is just that—God speaking to us. Every verse of the Bible is a personal invitation to listen to the voice of our Creator. Every time we open the Bible we open ourselves for an encounter with God. Our time with the Word of God is not for the mere acquisition of knowledge. It should be the basis of a continuing dialogue with Him that will actually shape our experience of daily living. I have found there are four steps to forming this dialogue through praying the scriptures: First, reading with open ears, "Speak, LORD; for thy servant heareth" (1 Sam. 3:9). Second, meditating with open heart, "thou shalt seek the LORD thy God, thou shalt find him, if thou seek him with all thy heart and with all thy soul" (Deut. 4:29). Third, waiting with open mind, "I wait for the LORD, my soul doth wait, and in his word do I hope" (Ps. 130:5). Fourth, responding with open hands, "I heard the voice of the Lord, saying, Whom shall I send, and who will go for us? Then said I, Here am I; send me" (Isa. 6:8).

Taking the first step, reading with open ears, means we will read slowly and thoughtfully, sometimes meditating on each word, letting the meaning of each phrase sink into our mind, none of this "in one ear and out the other" stuff. The words of Scripture are to be tasted, weighed, heard—in other words, experienced with all our senses—until a word, phrase, or sentence strikes us in some way—until something illumines us inside. Something will say, "Wow! that's neat. This is important." That "Wow!" moment is God talking to your heart, telling you something important for your life right now.

You may read two or three sentences or two or three chapters before that happens. (But I find most often it's only a few verses.) Whenever the "Wow" strikes, though, go no farther. You may wish to read the same passage over two or three times, but don't go on. That is God's Word for you today. It's time to move on to the second step and begin meditating with an open heart. Spend the rest of the day treasuring what God has said to you. Write it on a small card and slip it in your pocket, or put it on a sticky tab over your desk or sink as I do. But whatever your method, take the message with you throughout your day. Keep repeating it. This is God's Word working "effectually . . . in you" (1 Thess. 2:13).

One way to fix an inspiring thought in your mind is to share it with another person. At our house afternoon tea is a ritual. And part of the ritual is the race to see who can get their sharing on the table first. The first one with a stack of books or notes by his or her place gets to share first. Another example is my daughter's friend Megan who found such richness in the book of prayers she was reading this summer that she E-mailed one every day to her circle of friends.

Praying scripture is more than just a matter of letting God tell us things. Often we are reminded that prayer is two-way communication, so we must be quiet and let God talk to us. This is the third step of being still and knowing that He is God. In her book *Seeking God,* Esther De Waal says that prayer is the very heart of life. Prayer "holds everything together, it sustains every other activity. It is at the same time root and fruit, foundation and fulfillment. . . . It is the one thing that makes all the rest possible."[2] For the Christian, praying can never be set apart from the rest of life, it is life itself. When praying the scriptures the discipline is to be silent and listen. We cannot hear the Word until we are silent. Esther De Waal says, "Unless I am silent I shall not hear God, and until I hear him I shall not come to know him."[3]

And finally we come to the step of responding with open hands. We need to remember that when God speaks to us we owe Him the courtesy of responding. So as you go about your day meditating on your special word from God, talk to Him. Ask Him to show you how to apply your new insight or to show you answers to the questions it may have raised, or thank Him for His leading or assurance. But be prepared—this open communication with God may lead to more than talking. Full obedience to God may require action on your part—acts of charity, reaching out to others, giving of your time or your resources. Hobbyists need not apply.

But what about dry spells? Are there ever times when God doesn't speak? I doubt it. But there are certainly times when I don't hear. So what do you do when the words seem unintelligible, distant, or dry? The answer here is the same as the answer I most often receive any other time I cry out, "God, what shall I do about this?"

Most often the answer is, "Hold steady." So for praying the scriptures—stay in the Word. Continue reading and praying regularly. Remember my friend who had to let her baby cry it out? God is there just the same. Soon you will feel Him again.

It has been said that Scripture should be the principal source of all Christian prayer. This can be true if we allow it to enter our heart and kindle the divine spark that dwells there. Scriptures can kindle sparks of thanksgiving, repentance, petition, praise, meditation. Time spent praying the scriptures is a time of personal interaction with God's Word; it is making time and space in our day to be with the sacred. And thus is His image formed in us through this intimate communication with Him and complete obedience to Him.

Prayer Guide
Praying to Be More like Him

1. What are the qualities of God for which you most rejoice in praising Him?

2. Which of these do you desire most to see reflected in your life?

3. How could your life be changed by having these qualities more manifest in you?

4. Record Matt. 6:33. Record Prov. 3:6. How can you follow these commandments better?

5. In order to choose which book of the Bible you will use to begin praying the scriptures, consider:

What book are you reading now for your daily devotions?

Do you have a favorite book?

Is there a book you've never really read carefully?

Is there a book you've been thinking you would like to reread?

Record your choice.

6. At the time of your regular devotions or at a time you choose especially for your "divine reading," begin reading in your chosen book of the Bible. Read slowly, savoring each word or phrase as God speaking directly to you. When something jumps out at you, stop reading. Write it down.

7. Sit in silence for several minutes, thinking about this passage. What do you believe God is telling you?

8. Continue through your day meditating on this scripture and thinking about its special meaning to you. With what words or actions will you respond to God?

9. At the end of the day or next morning look back on your experience of praying scripture. Was your day any different? Are you any different?

10. Continue with this practice of praying the scriptures. Record your experiences in your prayer journal.

PART V

Praying

the High-Priestly Prayer Through Advent

Christ's High-Priestly Prayer

Father, the hour has come; Glorify Your Son, that Your Son also may glorify You, as You have given Him authority over all flesh, that He should give eternal life to as many as You have given Him. And this is eternal life, that they may know You, the only true God, and Jesus Christ whom You have sent. I have glorified You on the earth. I have finished the work which You have given Me to do. And now, O Father, glorify Me together with Yourself, with the glory which I had with You before the world was.

I have manifested Your name to the men whom You have given Me out of the world. They were Yours, You gave them to Me, and they have kept Your word. Now they have known that all things which You have given Me are from You. For I have given to them the words which You have given Me; and they have received them, and have known surely that I came forth from You; and they have believed that You sent Me. I pray for them. I do not pray for the world but for those whom You have given Me, for they are Yours. And all Mine are Yours, and Yours are Mine, and I am glorified in them. Now I am no longer in the world, but these are in the world, and I come to You. Holy Father, keep through Your name those whom You have given Me, that they may be one as We are. While I was with them in the world, I kept them in Your name. Those whom You gave Me I have kept; and none of them is lost except the son of perdition, that the Scripture might be fulfilled. But now I come to You, and these things I speak in the world, that they may have My joy fulfilled in themselves. I have given them Your word; and the world has hated them because they are not of the world, just as I am not of the world. I do not pray that You should take them out of the world, but that You should keep them from the evil one. They are not of the world, just as I am not of the world. Sanctify them by Your truth. Your word is truth. As You sent Me into the world, I also have sent them into the world. And for their sakes I sanctify Myself, that they also may be sanctified by the truth.

I do not pray for these alone, but also for those who will believe in Me through their word; that they all may be one, as You, Father, are in Me, and I in You; that they also may be one in Us, that the world may believe that You sent Me. And the glory which You gave Me I have given them, that they may be one just as We are one: I in them, and You in Me; that they may be made perfect in one, and that the world may know that You have sent Me, and have loved them as You have loved Me.

Father, I desire that they also whom You gave Me may be with Me where I am, that they may behold My glory which You have given Me; for You loved Me before the foundation of the world. O righteous Father! The world has not known You, but I have known You; and these have known that You sent Me. And I have declared to them Your name, and will declare it, that the love with which You loved Me may be in them, and I in them.

John 17, NKJV

18

The First Week of Advent: O Come, O Come, Emmanuel

All the comings and goings surrounding Christmas preparations—do they irritate you or stimulate you? Are they a frustration or a joy? Probably some of both. I'm certainly delighted to see family and friends during the holidays. But, honestly, some days I'd much rather sit by the Christmas tree and read or drink a cup of tea than have to go somewhere.

Did you ever think that most of the participants in the Christmas story must have felt the same way? Comings and goings at Christmastime are not unique to the modern world. Just consider: The angel came to Mary, Mary went to Elizabeth, Mary and Joseph went to Bethlehem, the angels came to the shepherds, the shepherds went to the manger, the wise men traveled hundreds of miles. And that doesn't even include the rigors of the flight into Egypt. The next time you're annoyed by having to make yet another trip to the mall, perhaps it will help to consider that at least you don't have to make the journey on a camel or a donkey.

But, of course, the greatest journey of all, was the coming to earth of the King of Glory. That is the point of all this activity that is so often decried as being worldly and pagan—something in human nature realizes a great event is about to happen all over again—Jesus Christ is coming in a new and fresh way—just as He has done every year for 2,000 years. And we have to do something. We have to get ready.

And so, as the calendar year winds down, we come to the beginning of a whole new year in the Christian calendar. The season of Advent—that glorious time when the world prepares anew for the coming of its Savior. But even more than preparation—with its emphasis on working and doing things and getting ready, Advent is about waiting—waiting for the longed-for Messiah who would save His people.

Our world isn't much into waiting. As a matter-of-fact, instant gratification is one of the hallmarks of today's society. "But I have to have it right now" is not a scriptural concept. The Bible teaches waiting in faith that God will fulfill His promises in His time. I know, I know—I'm one of those people who want everything yesterday, and with Calvin of Calvin and Hobbes often feel I could run through the house screaming because it's already half an hour later than it was half an hour ago—especially when I've got so much to do to get ready for Christmas. But that's not God's way of keeping time. And so, while all those around us are losing their heads in the frenzy of Christmas parties and Christmas shopping and Christmas decorations, and all the other frivolities (frivolous, yet in their own way important), we will attempt to keep our heads and our hearts and the season by concentrating on its real meaning and making a spiritual journey just as Mary and Joseph and all the others made an earthly journey to prepare for the first Christmas.

A call to repentance and a sense of expectancy are keynotes of the season. Four Sundays in Advent always precede Christmas Day; and Advent Sunday, the first day of Advent, is the day on which the ecclesiastical year begins. The first observance of the season seems to have been in Gaul in the sixth century—which makes Advent one of the last seasons of the Christian year for which a special observance was developed. At that time Advent was the end of the church year as well as the secular year and its special emphasis was on the second coming of Christ. Originally special services were held on the five Sundays, Wednesdays, and Fridays preceding Christmas. Traditionally Advent was a penitential season kept as Lent, but with less strictness. Fasting during Advent is no longer customary, although the penitential character of the season is marked by the use of the color purple.

Central to the observance of Advent is the Advent wreath, and I've been delighted to note the resurgence of popularity this ancient custom has enjoyed in recent years. Like most Christian customs, the Advent wreath is an adaptation of a pagan custom. Candles were lighted around a wheel during the winter solstice as a prayer that the sun might return again. Today our prayer is that the Son might renew our hearts. By the Middle Ages lighted candles and a wreath of evergreens had become integral parts of European Christmas celebrations.

The Advent wreath has a variety of symbolic meanings. The circular shape symbolizes eternity or the ever-renewing cycle of the seasons. The evergreens mean everlasting life. The greatest variety of meaning comes in the choice of candle colors. Purple candles are the most traditional, representing penance and longing, with one rose-colored candle to symbolize joy, although some churches use red candles for the blood of Christ's salvation. However, the center candle, the Christ candle, is always white, for the purity of Christ. Whatever the color of the candles, the flame symbolizes Jesus—the Light of the World. Advent wreaths can be used in your church, home, or study group—or better yet—all three.

In the first place, though, amid all the comings and goings involved in shopping, decorating, cooking, and visiting, must be taking time to prepare your heart for the most important coming of all. For this special season we will be working with the prayer Christ prayed for His disciples before He made another journey—the journey to the Cross. We will pray for the preparation of our hearts, our family, our community, and our world for the coming of Christ by praying Christ's intercessory prayer.

EMMANUEL SHALL COME TO THEE

The angel's announcement to Mary must have been one of the most shocking announcements of human history. And yet Mary responded, after an initial question, "Behold the handmaid of the Lord; be it unto me according to thy word" (Luke 1:38). Amazing acceptance. Amazing submission. But truly, the only reply really possible for one who proclaims Jehovah God as Lord of his or her life. A friend of mine remarked recently that he is always amused at Peter's reply in Acts 10:13 following his vision of the unclean beasts and the instruction to eat them. Peter said, "No, Lord." My friend says no true believer can say those two words in the same breath. One does not say no to one's Lord. Mary understood this.

And so must we understand that complete submission to the will of God is the key to praying the high-priestly prayer as preparation for Christ to come to our hearts in a new way this Advent season. We can have no greater example than the One who prayed this prayer, as it was prayed in preparation for His submission to the Cross. Christmas can have a whole new meaning for us; it can be the first Christmas all over again as we examine our hearts and renew our commitment in complete submission to His will.

Christ, who was about to abolish the high-priestly office and sacrifices by His death on the Cross, performed the function of an earthly high priest by praying for His disciples—and for all of us. It has been said that this prayer, found in the 17th chapter of the Gospel of John, contains the easiest words and the deepest meaning of any chapter in the Bible.

As Jesus began by praying for himself (vv. 1-5), we will begin our Advent study of this classic prayer by praying for ourselves, by preparing our hearts so that when we sing "Come, O Come, Emmanuel" our hearts will be ready for a fresh encounter with Him.

Notice first Christ's outward expression of fervent desire when He prayed; He "lifted up his eyes to heaven." The Bible commentator Matthew Henry says this is symbolic of lifting up one's soul to God in prayer. As the psalmist says, "Unto thee, O LORD, do I lift up my soul" (Ps. 25:1). Since early in the third century one of the highest moments of a traditional Communion service is the Sursum Corda, when the celebrant says, "Lift up your hearts." And the people reply, "We lift them up unto the Lord." At this moment the congregation is symbolically entering into the presence of God to worship "with Angels and Archangels, and with all the company of heaven." So can we, by expressing our intention, direct our souls to God in prayer.

It is significant that Christ began with prayer for himself before going on to pray for His disciples, the world, and all future believers. Notice the things Christ prays for himself: He prays that He might be glorified so that He can glorify God, and He prays to finish His work. Those two petitions are so comprehensive they take my breath away. I can think of nothing more I could possibly ask for.

Matthew Henry says this shows us what to aim at in our prayers and in all our designs and desires, "And that is, the honour of God. It being our chief end to glorify God, other things must be sought and attended to in subordination and subservience to the Lord. . . . 'Hallowed be thy name must be our first petition, which must fix our end in all our other petitions.'"[1]

Peter puts it like this: "If any man speak, let him speak as the oracles of God; if any man minister, let him do it as of the ability which God giveth: that God in all things may be glorified through Jesus Christ, to whom be praise and dominion for ever and ever. Amen" (1 Pet. 4:11).

Prayer Guide
Come to My Heart, Lord Jesus

1. Just as you make a list of the gifts you have to buy, the foods you have to prepare, the events you have to attend to get ready for Christmas, make a list of the spiritual preparations you need to make.

2. How do you plan to make time in your schedule this month to prepare for the coming of Christ?

3. Read John 17. Notice the four areas Christ's prayer covers and record some of the things He asks for each:
   - *a.* for himself (vv. 1-5)
   - *b.* for the disciples (vv. 6-19, 24-26)
   - *c.* for all believers (vv. 20-23)
   - *d.* for the world (vv. 21-23)

4. Rewrite vv. 1-5 as a prayer for yourself. Example: "Father, let Your Spirit come to me so that I might be able to glorify You. Let me live so that more people can come to know You. Help me to fulfill the work You have for me. Help me to reflect Your glory to the world around me."

5. List the things you can do to help this prayer be fulfilled.

6. Pray this prayer morning and evening through the first week of Advent. Picture in your mind God's glory shining on you and then reflecting to those around you. How might keeping this image before you affect your behavior?

7. End your devotional time by reading or singing "Come, Thou Long-Expected Jesus." Personalize the pronouns as you meditate on the meaning of the words.

19

The Second Week of Advent: Now the Savior Long-Expected

"Prepare to meet thy God!" The preacher, in black robe and white wig, stood on a busy corner in London, gesturing broadly with his arms to help his words carry over the rattle of carriage wheels on the rutted street: "The unrighteous are in a deplorable case indeed. You are deservedly alarmed, for aught you know, you may receive a pre-emptory summons that you cannot ploy with—to walk into eternity in the twinkling of an eye, whether sleeping or waking, who can tell?

"Surely on the night of Wednesday, the fourth of April, or the morning of Thursday, the fifth of April, London will be destroyed by a third, this time, completely devastating earthquake." The preacher outside the Fleet Prison was only one of dozens on the streets of London proclaiming approaching doom that spring of 1750. Early in the year a devastating earthquake had struck Lisbon, Portugal, demolishing the city and killing thousands. One month later a violent earthquake shook London. When a second, much more severe quake leveled parts of London exactly a month later the frenzy reached even such notable thinkers as Sir Isaac Newton who predicted that Jupiter would approach so close to the earth as possibly to brush it. The noted astronomer Dr. Halley had even declared the imminent return of his fiery comet to be on a collision course with earth.

The date of the final, apocalyptic quake was predicted to be one month after the second. Earthquake mania reigned: Preachers proclaimed earthquake theology, earthquake sermons were widely circulated and avidly read, ladies gathered their servants to sew earthquake gowns of heavy white linen to be worn on the cataclysmic night.

When the day arrived, all who could gathered in parks and on greens and spent that April night singing hymns and awaiting their eternal judgment. John Wesley, however, records that he "went to bed at my usual time, and was fast asleep about ten o'clock."

That's one of my favorite end-of-the-world stories. And yet, in spite of the delicious absurdities of such accounts, an element of truth is inescapable. Ever since that faithful band of believers heard Christ say, "It is not for you to know the times or the seasons, which the Father hath put in his own power," and then watched as He ascended and a cloud received Him out of their sight we have awaited His return. And so we wait this Advent season, 2,000 years later.

Historically, Christians in Rome saw Advent as a time to prepare to celebrate Christ's first coming to earth and more fully surrender themselves to His Lordship in our lives. Christians in outlying areas of the empire, however, saw the season as one to focus on the second coming of Christ to our world. "Prepare to meet thy God" was a powerful theme for missionaries and evangelists—whether or not the land had just been struck by a series of earthquakes. It was not until the Middle Ages that the two traditions came together in Christian worship with the more or less settled practice of emphasizing Christ's second coming to earth on the second Sunday of Advent.

Although the phrase *Second Coming* is not used in the Bible, *Nelson's Illustrated Bible Dictionary* records that there are over 300 references in the New Testament to the return of Christ. "The New Testament is filled with expectancy of His coming, even as Christians should be today."[1] Advent is a good time to renew that expectancy in our lives.

Throughout the history of Christianity there have been numerous interpretations of what is meant by the Second Coming, such as the coming of the Holy Spirit on the Day of Pentecost, Christ's coming to the heart at conversion, or even Christ's coming for the believer at the time of death. The clearest understanding, however, is that Christ's second coming will be a climactic historical event—far beyond the cataclysm of any earthquake.

Charles Wesley expressed the excitement of expecting the return of our Savior and King in a hymn that is often sung on the second Sunday of Advent:

> *Lo, He comes with clouds descending,*
> *Once for favored sinners slain;*
> *Thousand thousand saints attending*
> *Swell the triumph of His train.*
> *Hallelujah! Hallelujah!*
> *God appears on earth to reign.*
>
> *Ev'ry eye shall now behold Him,*
> *Robed in dreadful majesty!*
> *Those who set at naught and sold Him,*
> *Pierced, and nailed Him to the tree,*
> *Deeply wailing, deeply wailing,*
> *Shall the true Messiah see.*

Now the Savior, long-expected,
See in solemn pomp appear.
All His saints, by man rejected,
Now shall meet Him in the air.
Hallelujah! Hallelujah!
See the day of God appear.

Yes, amen! let all adore Thee,
High on Thine eternal throne;
Savior, take the pow'r and glory,
Claim the kingdom for Thine own.
O come quickly! O come quickly!
Everlasting God, come down!

It is appropriate, then, to make the return of the Lord a matter of constant expectancy and preparation. We must live in a state of constant readiness for anything God's timetable requires—including the end of time. And we must do all that we can to help others be prepared as well. This week we will focus especially on helping our families be prepared.

MY JOY FULFILLED IN THEM

This was going to be the best December our family had ever had. I really had it all together this time. Some friends and I had even written a whole booklet of skits, readings, and activities for family Advent times and distributed it to our church. The activities featured an Advent wreath (which I had made), a Nativity scene (which I had set up), a map (which I had tacked to the wall), and costumes (which I had assembled). My realistic husband was skeptical, but willing. The ever-romantic optimist, I was certain of success. Our sons, ages 11, 8, and 4, had not been still long enough to offer an opinion.

"Now, look: Stanley will light the first two candles on the wreath, Preston will put Mary and Joseph and the donkey at the far end of the table, and John will put the figures on the map. Then we'll all put on these neat costumes and act out the story of Mary and Joseph traveling to Bethlehem . . ."

It should have worked great, really it should have. Other families reported fantastic success using the little blue booklet for cozy family evenings. Not one other mother in the church admitted to ending the evening in tears. Well, at least my family liked the hot chocolate and brownies the innkeeper served, and by that time I didn't care how scripturally inaccurate it was.

In case you've had similar experiences, let me encourage you not to abandon hope. I'm a slow learner—some might even say ineducable— so through the years I persisted with such episodes of insanity, often involving neighbors and other families. Calling in recruits was especially

necessary for such schemes as singing the "Hallalujah Chorus" when
caroling (a feat we never pulled off, even though our friends were very
musical). An evening of Victorian carols—in costume, of course—was
much more successful. At least we looked good. But I'm happy to report
that a couple of Christmases ago with the help of a new daughter-in-law
with a degree in drama, talented neighbors, and brave distant relatives
we successfully managed a full three-act play in our basement for the
festive season.

All of which is to illustrate the importance of times of family fun
and family preparation and family prayer as we approach the coming of
Christ. My favorite use of Christ's prayer for His disciples is to pray it for
my family—sometimes for them as a group, sometimes for an individual child. I have done this for a number of years ever since I was first
struck with the similarities of Jesus' feelings for the disciples He was
about to leave and my feelings for my children. This is especially so now
that our family is older and partings occur so often.

As I look back through my journal I find numerous paraphrases,
meditations, and poems I have written for my children based on Christ's
prayer. An adult child moving to a foreign country, an adolescent child
facing surgery, a growing-up child falling in love . . . these are some of
the intense moments of life when I didn't have the words I needed to
pray, but Jesus had already said them for me.

Dear Father, protect my children in Your name. Make them one
with You and with each other. You have given us Your name that we
may be one as Father, Son, and Spirit are One. When they were
home their father and I protected them in Your name. We guarded
them, and not one was lost.

Make your joy complete in them. We taught them your Word.
The world hates those that do not belong to the world, but we don't
ask You to take them out of the world, rather to protect them from
the evil one. They do not belong to this world as You do not belong
to this world.

Sanctify them in the truth. Your Word is truth. You have sent
them into the world. You gave yourself for them that they may be
sanctified in truth.

In Your holy name, let Your kingdom come to earth and Your
will be done here as in heaven through my children. Lead them not
into temptation. Protect them from evil. For thine is the kingdom
and the power and the glory for ever and ever. Amen. (Written in the
chapel of St. Alphonsus Hospital.)

Here, as always, my prayer was not far from the Lord's Prayer, either. I have also written the prayer in similar form inserting the name of
a specific child. Sometimes I sent the prayer to that child; and sometimes, like Mary, I've kept it in my heart.

When one of my children found their heart seriously engaged I used petitions from Christ's prayer for His disciples as the basis for a prayer poem for these two beautiful young people:

That They May Be One

They are Yours.
They have received Your Word.
Keep them in Your Word
That they may be one in Your Word
And Your joy be fulfilled in them.

Keep them from evil.
They are not of the world,
They have been sanctified through Your Truth
That they may be one in Truth
And Your joy fulfilled in them.

As Father and Son are one
Let them be one in Father and Son
That the world may see You in them.
You have given them Your glory
That they may be one in Your glory
And Your joy fulfilled in them.

You in them
And them in You
That they may be made perfect in one,
That the world may know You through them
And see Your love in them.
That the love of the Father may be in them
And Christ in them
That they may be one in Your love
And Your joy fulfilled in them.

Using this prayer for our families lays a heavy responsibility on the pray-er, however. Look carefully at Christ's model. Note how He uses His own behavior as a model for what He asks the Father to do for His disciples: "I have glorified thee, . . . I have manifested thy name, . . . I pray for them, . . . I have given them thy word." These are all actions we must model to those for whom we pray. We, of course, will never match Christ's perfection, but as His followers we should do our best even to not being of the world, but being sanctified, or set apart, by being "oned" with the Father. A heavy responsibility—a glorious prospect.

Prayer Guide
Come to My Family, Lord Jesus

1. One of the hallmarks of good poetry or hymnody is the use of concrete

images, helping the reader or singer picture touchable things in order to teach concepts. Reread carefully "Lo, He Comes with Clouds Descending" and list the vivid images.

2. Read John 14:3; Acts 1:11; 1 Thess. 4:16; Rev. 1:7; 22:20. What do these verses teach you about Christ's second coming?

3. Read the parable Christ taught about His return in Matt. 25:1-13. It is significant that this is Jesus' last public discourse before His crucifixion—and He chose to teach on the Second Coming. One meaning suggested here is that the lamp is faith and that the oil is love—therefore, a lamp with oil in it is faith working by love. In this light, how can you apply the parable to your life?

4. Most of us have our hands full dealing with life today, but how might a greater awareness that Christ will return change some of the things you do?

5. What things do you do to make Christmas memorable for your family?

6. What can you do to make Christmas more spiritual for your family?

7. Read John 17:6-19, 24-26. What does Jesus say He has done for His disciples? What does He say about the disciples? What does He ask the Father to do for the disciples?

8. What do you most want to do for your family? What do you most want God to do for them?

9. Using Christ's prayer for His disciples as a model, write a prayer, poem, or meditation for your family in your journal. Pray it every day this week.

20

The Third Week of Advent: Joyful, Joyful, We Adore Thee

The pictures of our new grandson arrived the other day—not the electronic ones that come out faded and grainy when you print them, but honest-to-goodness glossy photographs that I can hold in my hand and take to church and the grocery store and the beauty parlor and bore everyone to death with—that is, anyone who is insensitive enough not to appreciate such amazing beauty. But seriously, the thing that overwhelmed me as I looked at the pictures of my 32-year-old firstborn son holding his two-week-old first son was the look of absolute adoration on Stanley's face. And knowing the great joy little Thomas had brought to all our lives I suddenly put it together: Adoration brings joy to the adorer.

Think about it—the joy of adoring a baby, the joy of adoring one's beloved, the joy of adoring beauty in nature or art, the joy of adoring God. That's what the joy of Christmas is all about—adoring Jesus. And that's what the third Sunday of Advent is about—joy. That's why the candle for this week is rose, the color symbolizing joy; and that's why Mary is the focus of many meditations this week, because she was the first to adore Him.

The third Sunday in Advent is sometimes called Gaudete Sunday, *Gaudete* being the Latin imperative—Rejoice! or even the command, "You all rejoice!" Traditionally, the entrance song for this Sunday is Phil. 4:4, "Rejoice in the Lord alway: and again I say, Rejoice."

The thing to remember about joy is that it's a quiet emotion. It is an almost solemn ecstasy that starts deep within one, filling with a radiance that finally works itself into shining eyes and an irrepressible smile. Joy is easily drowned in noise and rush. We lose the joy of the season in busyness. Fun is not joy. Or, as William Stringfellow says in *The Services of the Christian Year,* "For all the greeting-card and sermonic rhetoric, much rejoicing does not seem to happen around Christmastime, least of all about the coming of the Lord. There is a lot of holiday frolicking, but that is not the same as rejoicing."[1]

There is much wisdom in the simple hymn "O Come, Let Us Adore Him." Let us focus on holding Him quietly in our hearts and adoring Him this week, that our joy may be full.

There is an interesting quality about joy. You can't contain it. Real joy has a bouyant quality that just bubbles over, so it's appropriate that our emphasis this week is praying the Disciples' Prayer for all believers, starting with our own church and then for Christians around the world. Notice what Christ prays for His Church, not once, not twice, not three times, but four times in three verses: "That they all may be one; as thou, Father, art in me, and I in thee, that they also may be one in us . . . that they may be one, even as we are one . . . that they may be perfect in one." So should we pray for a spirit of love, unity, and peace for all believers.

THAT THEY MAY BE ONE

My husband walked in the door. "Donna, we've got to talk." My immediate thought was that I had dented his car—nothing else could make him look so austere. Actually, the news was far graver than that. In five days I was to fly to Northern Ireland. The blessed peace of the 18-month-long ceasefire had just been shattered by a bomb in London.

"Go ahead with dinner," I said. "I'm going upstairs to pray—and I'm not coming down until I have an answer." The message was clear—this could take all night.

I was back in the kitchen in less than 10 minutes. "Mom, what are you doing here?"

"It's all right. There was nothing to pray about. The Lord promised His peace."

We were fine, but in Ireland I saw on every hand the devastation that comes when Christians fail to dwell together in unity. People were physically ill at the thought that they would have to return to the tension, fear, and destruction that they had known through 30 years of sectarian strife.

Across Ireland, both north and south, the people gathered on greens and in city squares, wearing white ribbons, signing petitions, and rallying for peace. In a park near Dublin we sang "Bring Us Together, Lord" before the speaker declared, "Peace is possible!" The crowd cheered at his opening. "But we must seek it at the right source—not in politics, not in arms, but in the One who has called us to live in peace and who will give us peace within ourselves to give to others and to spread over our land. When there is peace in the heart, there can be peace in the home. When there is peace in the home, there can be peace in the community. When there is peace in the community, there can be peace in the nation." If you've read a newspaper recently, you know that Ireland is just one land where such peace isn't a reality yet. All Christians are not yet one. We have not embraced one another as brothers and sisters in Christ. So we need to keep working and praying and loving. And what better time to focus on this need than now when we prepare for the coming of the Prince of Peace. I'm a firm believer in the importance of theology, of denominational distinctives. God's truth is too great for any one mind, any one church, or any one denomination to understand or to be able to proclaim it all. That's why so many kinds of churches exist—because there's more than enough truth to go around. We all have a shard of the Truth. (Of course, I believe my own church happens to have a larger shard than some.) But someday—in heaven—all those shards will fit together to make an unbelievably beautiful stained-glass window through which the eternal sun will shine.

Until that day, however, we need to do our part to bring about the oneness that Christ prayed for. I am one with all who profess Christ as Lord, who hold to the essentials of the faith as outlined in the historic creeds of the universal church. One of the best places to begin expressing this communion is by adoring Christ together and rejoicing together in His birth. Most communities seem to sense this as so many ecumenical services, pageants, prayer vigils, and concerts are held this time of year. Lending our support to such efforts can be a step toward fulfilling Christ's vision.

In this same spirit, "The Prayers of the People" from the *Book of Common Prayer* begin with these words, "Let us pray for the whole state of Christ's Church and the world." The first petition then beseeches God "to inspire continually the universal Church with the spirit of truth, unity, and concord; and grant that all those who do confess thy holy Name may agree in the truth of thy holy Word, and live in unity and godly love." The congregation then prays for the leaders of their church and other ministers, and then for themselves, "to all thy people give thy heavenly grace, and especially to this congregation here present; that, with meek heart and due reverence, they may hear and receive thy holy Word, truly serving thee in holiness and righteousness all the days of their life." Much could be accomplished if all Christians made such a prayer a regular, fervent cry of their heart.

Prayer Guide
Come, O Lord, to Your Church

1. Charles Wesley wrote a hymn on Phil. 4:4, "Rejoice, the Lord is King; Your Lord and King adore! / Rejoice, give thanks, and sing, And triumph evermore. / Lift up your heart; Lift up your voice! / Rejoice; again I say: rejoice!" Sing or meditate on this hymn. How does the act of adoration lead to rejoicing?

2. Read Isa. 12:2-6. Why does the prophet say we should rejoice in the Lord?

3. The Psalms are full of rejoicings. Some of my favorite are 5:11; 9:1-2; 20:5, and especially 95 through 100. Spend time rejoicing with the psalmist. Record some of your favorite references or verses.

4. Read John 17:20-23. What does Christ ask the Father to do for all believers?

5. What are some needs of your local congregation for which you are especially praying?

6. What are some needs of the church around the world for which you pray regularly?

7. In the last few years Christians have become especially aware of the importance of praying for the persecuted church. List some world areas where Christianity is suppressed and Christians persecuted.

8. One of the worst tragedies of humankind and the greatest triumphs of Satan is Christians persecuting, or just backbiting, each other—even in our own country, our own church. List some examples of this.

9. When we pray for the universal Church we are praying not only for those alive right now but also for those who have gone before us and for those yet to come. List some Christians of past ages for whom you are especially thankful.

Pray that their influence will continue to be felt. What do you want God to do for future generations of Christians?

10. Using the model of "The Prayers of the People" quoted on page 133, write a prayer for the universal Church in your journal. Pray it every day this week.

The Fourth Week of Advent: Our Hope Is in the Coming of the Lord

O come, O come, Emmanuel, / And ransom captive Israel, / That mourns in lowly exile here / Until the Son of God appear. / Rejoice! Rejoice! Emmanuel / Shall come to thee, O Israel!" This is the ultimate Advent hymn. How we love to sing "O come, Thou Dayspring, come and cheer / Our spirits by Thine advent here. / Disperse the gloomy clouds of night, / And death's dark shadows put to flight . . . / Fill the whole world with heaven's peace." Even though the minor key of the melody expresses longing, few words could be more hopeful. And that's the message of Advent, the proclamation that "our hope is in the coming of the Lord."

Hope in the Lord. Easy, even elevating, to say; but hard to understand. *Hope* is such a slippery term. Like the word *love,* we use it freely for thoughts and feelings of various intensity—and by so doing vitiate its truly deepest meanings. Hope is longing, anticipation, belief, desire . . . all of those and more.

Entire theologies have been built on the concept of hope. *The Oxford Dictionary of the Christian Church* defines *hope* as "the desire and search for a future good, difficult but not impossible of attainment." Hope is a key concept throughout the Old Testament, often with an emphasis on material security as well as religious desires. The most intense hope, of course, was the longing of the nation of Israel for the Messiah. In the New Testament we read of our hope of salvation through Jesus Christ.

Theologians of the Early Church divided virtues into theological and natural virtues. The natural virtues: prudence, temperance, fortitude, and justice were first enunciated by the pre-Christian Greek thinkers Plato and Aristotle; whereas the theological virtues faith, hope, and love are delineated in the New Testament by the apostle Paul. Hope's primary end, its motive, and its author is God himself, and like faith it may continue even when charity has been lost by human sinning. Hope, *The Oxford Dictionary of the Christian Church* concludes, "being

135

confidence in God's goodness tempered by fear of His justice, is op-posed to both despair and presumption."

OK, that's all really good stuff—after all, I got it from books written by really brilliant people—and it does help me understand what we mean when we say, "Our hope is in the coming of the Lord." But I'm a very right-brained person. I have to take abstract theology in very small doses. The concrete images the psalmist gives us of what it means to hope in the Lord are more useful to me:

> Happy is he who has the God of Jacob for his help, whose hope is in the LORD his God, who made heaven and earth, the sea, and all that is in them; who keeps truth forever, who executes justice for the oppressed, who gives food to the hungry. The LORD gives free-dom to the prisoners. The LORD opens the eyes of the blind; the LORD raises those who are bowed down; the LORD loves the righ-teous. The LORD watches over the strangers; he relieves the father-less and widow; but the way of the wicked He turns upside down. The LORD shall reign forever—your God, O Zion, to all generations. Praise the LORD! *(Ps. 146:5-10, NKJV).*

This is our hope, this is our God—the One who created all, who keeps truth forever, who executes justice, gives food and freedom, heals the blind, raises the weary, loves the righteous, watches over strangers and orphans, rebuffs the wicked—and reigns forever. Amen! At mo-ments like this I truly understand why I'm an evangelical—don't you just want to rush out and share that with everyone! Isn't that exactly what our world needs! And He is coming, and He has come, and He will come again! And that's why, in the last week of Advent, we pray, as Christ did in His prayer, for the whole world, that all might discover the unspeakable riches of His coming.

Queen Berthe is a wonderful example of one who lived in constant, persevering hope for 35 years—the hope referred to in Rom. 8:25, hop-ing for the unseen and waiting in patience.

In the year 562 Berthe, daughter of the Christian king of Paris, came to Canterbury to marry the heathen Anglo-Saxon King Ethelbert. The marriage agreement included the provision that Berthe would be al-lowed to continue Christian worship with her own priest. On a hillside outside the city was the tiny, ruined church of St. Martin's that had been a place of Christian worship during Roman times. It was to this church that Queen Berthe and her ladies made their way through the city gate, past heathen shrines, and up the steep hill every day in all weather, to pray without ceasing for the conversion of King Ethelbert, of England, and of its people.

After 35 years of such faithfulness Augustine came as a missionary to England. The King and all the land became Christian. Berthe's hope was fulfilled.

Pray the Lord of the Harvest

Several years ago I had an experience that has given me hope to pray with some of Berthe's faithfulness for the revival that our world so desperately needs today. It was September and we were flying from Glasgow to London. Miracle of miracles—it wasn't raining. Almost the entire length of the island I had a clear view of the land below, and unique to that time of year, it was not the green, green land I so cherish, but rather field after field of gold.

The thought struck me with such force that I cried hard enough to scare my daughter sitting beside me—but the clear image and accompanying words has never left me—the fields were ripe unto harvest.

This experience was reinforced a few months later when I was teaching at a writing school for a missionary organization and they gave me a prayer calendar with the picture of a man standing looking out at a ripe wheat field waiting to be harvested. And the field was the shape of Africa. Again I was struck by the scriptural injunction, "Behold, I say unto you, Lift up your eyes, and look on the fields; for they are white already to harvest" (John 4:35). "The harvest truly is plenteous, but the labourers are few" and so we must pray to "the Lord of the harvest, that he will send forth labourers into his harvest" (Matt. 9:37-38).

And for this prayer we have Christ's model in His high-priestly prayer. Twice He prayed for the oneness of the disciples, for God's glory to be seen in the disciples, even for the perfection of the disciples that the world may believe. It's all very well—even important—for us to pray for one another as believers, but we need to remember that the love and joy we share together in the Lord isn't for its own sake, but rather "that the world may know that thou hast sent me, and hast loved them, as thou hast loved me" (John 17:23).

Matthew Henry says in his commentary on this passage, "When Christianity, instead of causing quarrels about itself, makes all other strifes to cease—when it cools the fiery, smooths the rugged, and disposes men to be kind and loving, courteous and beneficent, to all men, studious to preserve and promote peace in all relations and societies, this will recommend it to all."[1]

Then the world will know that Christ's "doctrine was divine, in that his religion prevails to join so many of different capacities, tempers, and interests in other things, in one body by faith, with one heart by love." When we are truly one, then the world "will be ready to say, We will go with you, for we see that God is with you."[2]

Studying these verses the week before Christmas can give a new meaning to John 3:16-17, "For God so loved the world, that he gave his only begotten Son, that whosoever believeth in him should not perish, but have everlasting life. For God sent not his Son into the world to condemn the world; but that the world through him might be saved." Be-

cause these verses are part of Christ's teaching about His coming crucifixion we tend to associate them more with the Easter season, but they
are equally—if not even more—appropriate for this time as we prepare
to celebrate God's sending His Son into the world as a babe in a manger.

So this week we pray for all the world—that all people will open
their hearts to the coming of Christ. That the world will see Him and
know Him for their Savior. That true, heart-changing revival will come to
our world. That, as we prayed during Lent, His will will be done as completely on earth as it is in heaven.

And, of course, we want it now—but that's only because we didn't
get it yesterday. And such feelings are justified, because every day people die, every day there are disasters, every day people need God's help.
Queen Berthe must have often felt the same way. Why was the Spirit de-
laying when so many people needed God in their lives right then? Certainly, I don't know the answer to that. But I do know that we are to hold
on, and I know that preparation is essential for any endeavor—that's
what Advent is all about. And so we can make part of our Advent
preparing for a great revival—in God's perfect time.

Sometimes I think of praying for revival as stacking brushwood—
just piling up a great heap of dry sticks, or to be more precise—since I
live surrounded by desert—of sagebrush. Once I was complaining a bit
because the land still seemed so spiritually dry and thirsty (you know,
the "How long, O Lord, how long?" sort of complaining that Queen
Berthe must have been tempted to indulge in once in awhile), and the
Lord reminded me that dry brush burns the best. The drier and deader it
is, the quicker it will catch fire when God sends the torchbearer.

So, as we pray, we wait in hope. As Paul says in Rom. 8:24, "For in
hope we were saved. Now hope that is seen is not hope. For who hopes
for what is seen? But if we hope for what we do not see, we wait for it
with patience" (author's paraphrase of the American Standard Version).

I've mentioned before that patience is not my strongest point, so at
the risk of mixing my metaphors, I want to share one more insight I had,
this one regarding my "fields ripe unto harvest" showing from the plane
window. I came to realize that, indeed, many fields were ripe—but not
all. Many were still green. Some were ready for the harvest of revival—
but not all. God knows when the fullness of time is come and when all
the fields are ready.

Besides, if we could bring revival—or anything else—by the ferven-
cy, frequency, or even longevity of our prayers, then the results would
not be of God's grace but of our works. This is really a very freeing
thought, for as much as I believe in the importance of prayer, I believe
even more that the results are God's. The salvation of the world is a
matter of God's grace—not of my work. And for that I am very, very
thankful. He has already done the work for us.

Part of having faith in the Lord of the harvest is believing that He
knows the right time to send the reapers into the field. And until then

we must be faithful to pray for His coming to our hearts and to our families and to our churches and to our world.

Prayer Guide
Come, O Lord, to All the World

1. The great Isaac Watts hymn "O God, Our Help in Ages Past" lists many things God does for us and reasons for us to hope in Him. Sing or read the hymn and list Watts's insights into serving a God of hope.

2. Study Rom. 8:18-25. List the things we are to hope for.

3. Read 1 Pet. 1:3-5, 8-9. Define the "living hope" God has given us.

4. The "theological virtues" faith, hope, and love are linked several times in Scripture. Read Col. 1:4-5 and 1 Thess. 1:3. What do these verses say about the object and result of these virtues?

5. Ps. 146:5 says that the person who hopes in the Lord is happy. What reasons does the psalmist give for this happiness?

6. When you pray "that the world may believe," what are you praying for? Are there particular world areas where you long to see revival?

7. If you could tell the world what you most want them to know, what would you say?

8. Write a prayer for the world in your journal. Pray it every day this week.

PART VI

Praying

the Canticles Through Christmas and Epiphany

The Magnificat

My soul magnifies the Lord,
And my spirit has rejoiced in God my Savior.
For He has regarded the lowly state of His maid-
    servant;
For behold, henceforth all generations will call me
    blessed.
For He who is mighty has done great things for
    me,
And holy is His name.
And His mercy is on those who fear Him from
    generation to generation.
He has shown strength with His arm;
He has scattered the proud in the imagination of
    their hearts.
He has put down the mighty from their thrones,
And exalted the lowly.
He has filled the hungry with good things,
And the rich He has sent away empty.
He has helped His servant Israel,
In remembrance of His mercy,
As He spoke to our fathers,
To Abraham and to his seed forever.

—Luke 1:47-55, NKJV

22

Unto You a Child Is Born

CHRISTMAS MIDNIGHT

Entranced in wonder, kneel by flickering light,
Bells chime of whispered snow, and one bright star
Tells joy this silent night, this holy night.

In star-capped apse the advent flames ignite,
While straw enfolds the Babe come from afar.
Entranced, in wonder kneel by flickering light—

Illumination's Truth enkindled bright.
Pine garlands green eternal life declare,
Telling of joy this silent, holy night.

At red-gold altar the Christ Child mass recite:
Take, eat the bread, of Grace a harbinger,
Entranced, in wonder kneel. By flickering light

Raise high the incensed prayers for God's delight,
Praise Him who comes, our King, our Counselor,
Bringing joy, this silent night. This holy night

Emmanuel is born anew. Blest rite,
The vigil keep on sacred calendar.
Entranced, in wonder kneel by flickering light,
Replete with joy this silent, holy night.

—D. F. C.

The peace and beauty permeating the poet's Christmas Eve is what we all search for in the midst of the holiday frenzy, and yet it is so hard to find—often even at church. Still, this is the true heart of Christmas. Whether it has been lost, or never truly found, I'm not certain. That it is desperately needed I can testify from my own experience.

With all the focus on Christmas and all the fuss surrounding it today, it is almost impossible for us to realize that it was the last of the Christian festivals to be added to the Church calendar. With perhaps a clearer grasp of the central focus of the gospel, early Christians made Easter the great festival of the year and the proclamation of the Resurrection the core of their message. The celebration of the anniversary of Christ's birth does not appear to have been a general practice among Christians until near the end of the fourth century, growing from the support of the Emperor Constantine. In some churches this great festival is celebrated with three services: at midnight, at the dawn, and in the day, symbolizing the threefold birth of Christ—eternally in the bosom of the Father, from the womb of the Virgin Mary, and mystically in the soul of the faithful.

Appropriately, Christians converted a pagan festival celebrating the yearly rebirth of the sun into celebrating the birth of the Son of God. Today, some would say that a Christian festival is being converted into a pagan one. But you know, it doesn't really bother me—all the hoopla around Christmas. It is all for the birth of Jesus—even if a lot of people *hoop*ing and *la*ing don't know it. It's our job to show them what it's really all about—and we don't do that by outhooping them. We show the world that Christmas is the birthday of the Prince of Peace by being peaceful. Our church services, our family gatherings, even our parties should reflect peace and joy and love, not irrational exuberance.

That may mean paring things down a bit to get to the heart of the matter. But you know, that first Christmas was pretty pared down: weary travelers, clean (we hope) straw, a few animals—and then glory broke through. We can follow the same pattern today: a gathering of family or friends—then worship. But don't wait until it's all quiet. "Silent Night" is everyone's favorite Christmas carol, but how silent could it all really have been 2,000 years ago—what with the town overrun with travelers partying in the inn, animals moving and snorting around the manger, angels singing, shepherds and goodness knows who else coming to gawk—all on top of a newborn baby to care for. I believe Mary and Joseph were peaceful—if exhausted—because they were focused on Christ. And they set a standard of beauty and worship that night that has never been equaled. Let's see what we can do to let some of it rub off on our own Christmas.

MAGNIFYING THE LORD

The sound of handbells rang through the cathedral, echoing in the high wooden hammered beams. The golden glow of evening illuminated the Tiffany window picturing angels surrounding Mary looking adoringly at the Christ child on her lap. I knelt in rapture, thinking this was as close to heaven as I was likely to get in this life. A few weeks before, my friend Betty had sent me a bulletin announcing "traditional English Evensong" at her church, and here I was experiencing perhaps the most beautiful worship service of the Anglican tradition—certainly the most peaceful.

"The Lord is in his holy temple: Let all the earth keep silence before him," the minister proclaimed, then sang, "O Lord, open Thou our lips."

"And our mouth shall show forth Thy praise," the small, scattered congregation and faithful, angelic choir responded. We sang the Gloria Patri and chanted a psalm, listened to a scripture reading, and then sang, "My soul doth magnify the Lord, and my spirit hath rejoiced in God my Savior . . ." I had never before sung the song that burst from Mary's heart in joy that she was to be the mother of the long-awaited Messiah, and my heart lifted and glorified God in Mary's words: "Holy is his name, and His mercy is on them that fear Him throughout all generations . . ."

This was a new experience in worshiping God—one I will never forget.

The Bible is full of canticles—beautiful songs that people of God sang when they were greatly moved by His majesty and goodness. Through the ages Christians have enhanced their own worship by repeating these words as their own songs of praise. The Magnificat is one of the most beautiful and frequently sung of the canticles. Various churches utilize different canticles in their worship. There are 44 Old Testament and 9 New Testament songs that are sung with some degree of regularity by Christians around the world. Since at least the sixth century, however, the Magnificat has been considered the canticle of the evening service of the Western church.

The language of Mary's hymn of praise is steeped in the poetic tradition of the Old Testament, and reflects another beautiful canticle, the Song of Hannah, with which Mary was undoubtedly familiar. Both women rejoice from their hearts in the mighty acts of God who has chosen to exalt a lowly handmaiden, scattering the proud, breaking the mighty, and raising up the poor—in Mary, as in Hannah, God was reversing human values. And yet the songs are very different, for Hannah makes no secret of her sense of triumph over those who had taunted her for years because of her childlessness; but Mary shows the qualities for which we still honor her today—her humility and her acceptance of God's will, even as she realizes the honor that has been thrust upon her. Mary sees herself as insignificant but realizes that the mighty God is at work.

Prophetically, Mary sang of Christ himself who would be born to save His people from their sins. Mary "rejoiced in hope of salvation through faith in Him, which is a blessing common to all true believers, more than in being His mother after the flesh." Because Mary sang of the universal experience, rather than that which was to be peculiar to her, we can all sing her song as our own. We have the same reason to rejoice in God the Savior that Mary had. "Because He had regarded the low estate of his handmaid—In like manner has He regarded our low estate; and vouchsafed to come and save her and us, when we were reduced to the lowest estate of sin and misery."[1]

The Magnificat is one of the world's great poems and one of the greatest hymns of the Church. As we pray this prayer hymn at Christmas, we can praise God in Mary's words for: His might, His holiness, His mercy, His faithfulness, His righteousness, His justice, and His wise judgments; and in so doing make our Christmas season even more full of the glory of His coming to earth as a babe.

Prayer Guide
Praising with Mary

1. Even if you don't usually do so, make plans to attend a worship service on Christmas Eve or Christmas Day. Record the experience in your journal.

2. What will you do this Christmas to make it peaceful, holy, joyful, and centered in Him?

3. Some of the most beautiful Old Testament canticles are the two Songs of Moses, Exod. 15:1-19 and Deut. 32:1-43; the Song of Habakkuk, Hab. 3:2-19; and the Song of Isaiah, Isa. 26:1-21. Read each of these. Record some of your favorite lines from each.

4. Some New Testament canticles are in Eph. 1:3-10; Phil. 2:6-11; Col. 1:12-20. List the qualities for which these hymns praise Christ.

5. Read the Magnificat in Luke 1:46-55. List the things for which Mary praises God.

6. Read Hannah's canticle in 1 Sam. 2:1-10. Note the similarities to and differences from Mary's song.

7. William Barclay quotes Stanley Jones as saying, "The Magnificat is the most revolutionary document in the world." List some revolutionary statements in Mary's song.

8. Mary's song of praise is sparked by the song with which her cousin Elizabeth greets her. Read Luke 1:42-45. Have you had an experience in which a relative or close friend's words have inspired you?

9. Try to imagine how you would have felt in Mary's place at that time in her life. Record your thoughts in your journal.

10. In your journal write your own song of praise to God for what He has done for you.

11. Pray the Magnificat as your own prayer each day this week, or chant it as we did the psalms.

The Nunc Dimittis

Lord, now lettest thou thy servant depart in
peace, according to thy word:
For mine eyes have seen thy salvation,
Which thou hast prepared before the face of all
people;
A light to lighten the Gentiles, and the glory of
thy people Israel.

—Luke 2:29-32

23 | The Feast of Epiphany

The speech choir, only slightly out of unison, proclaimed: "And the wise men, having heard Herod, went their way; and behold, the star which they had seen in the east, went before them, until it came and stood over where the child was. And seeing the star they rejoiced with exceeding great joy."

The crowned and robed wise men approached the costumed Mary and Joseph at the front of the church, knelt, and then, holding out their gold, frankincense, and myrrh, each sang a verse of "We Three Kings," the congregation joining in enthusiastically on the chorus.

No, it wasn't Christmas Eve, or the week before. It was a full 12 days after Christmas. It was the Eve of Epiphany. After the "Festival of Lights" enacted by our youth, which recounted the life of Christ, the conversion of Constantine, the Reformation, and other major events in church history down to "The Light of Christ in Our Midst"—the founding of our local church, we gathered in the church hall for a medieval feast that included eating roast beef and Yorkshire pudding and singing and acting out all the verses of "The Twelve Days of Christmas." We had decided to beat the Christmas rush by following the footsteps of early Christians. Instead of adding more events to the pre-Christmas rush, we extended the celebrating to include the ancient Feast of the Epiphany.

Christmas and Epiphany are the two great feasts of the Incarnation of Jesus Christ. Actually, Epiphany is the older of the two festivals. It is possible that as early as the second century Christians in Egypt chose January 6 to celebrate Christ's birth, His baptism, and the first miracle at Cana. Clement of Alexandria records that believers spent the night of January 5/6 as a vigil and the day itself as a festival of our Lord's baptism. By the second half of the fourth century Epiphany was celebrated in Gaul, and Augustine said that it was observed "throughout the world." In the fourth century Epiphany ranked with Easter and Pentecost as one of the three great festivals of the Church. By the mid-fifth century the Feast of Epiphany was celebrated in Rome as a commemoration of the visitation of the magi to the infant Christ child, a fitting conclusion to the Christmas season. By the middle ages the Christmas/Epiphany festival season had grown into the celebration of a full 12 days of Christmas with the lord of every medieval manor expected to provide feasting, actors, jugglers, and trained bear acts for all his serfs and freemen. (Twentieth-century Americans were not the first to secularize a holy day.)

The word *Epiphany* comes from the Greek word meaning "appearance." The appearance of the wise men coming to worship the Christ child is the first sign that Jesus came to the Gentiles as well as to the Jews. To this day the English sovereign follows the example of the magi and makes offerings of gold, frankincense, and myrrh in the Chapel Royal on Epiphany. And some churches extend the visitation aspect of Epiphany with the custom of having the minister visit and bless the homes of church members during the week of Epiphany.

More often Epiphany is observed as a festival of lights, commemorating the coming of Christ as the Light of the World, the shining of the Christmas star that led the wise men to worship Him, and our carrying His light forward into the darkness. In this way the season has come full circle because the dates for both Christmas and Epiphany were, at least in part, an attempt to counter secular festivities connected with the pagan festival of winter solstice. So we can sing with the wise men: "O star of wonder, star of night, / Star with royal beauty bright, / Westward leading, still proceeding, / Guide us to thy perfect light."

LET THY SERVANT DEPART IN PEACE

The ancient man, thin and stooped with age, his gray beard straggling in spots, his eyesight dimming, stood in the forecourt of the Temple. He had waited so long, been disappointed so many times. Today would undoubtedly be like all the others. And yet he would not give up hope. For had not the Spirit of the Lord God Jehovah promised him? Had not he, simple, ordinary man that he was, been promised that he would not taste of death until he had seen the long-awaited Messiah? And yet, how much longer could he wait? His limbs ached in the winter, his breath came short in the summer. He had been so certain today as he prayed at home, so certain that the Holy Spirit was telling him to go to the Temple. But there was nothing out of the ordinary here today. That young couple, obviously from the country, bringing their infant to the priests for circumcision—that could be any couple with any eight-day-old male son in Israel. Simeon's shoulders slumped as he turned away. How long, O Lord, how long? he cried with the prophet Isaiah.

Then he wondered if he had spoken aloud, for the gentle-looking young mother smiled at him as if in reply. Simeon blinked to clear his sight. Had he been praying with such intensity that he had brought on an illusion? No, the vision was accompanied by the very real weight of the infant the woman placed in his arms. Soft, warm, lively—and infinitely precious. And Simeon knew that he held the Savior in his arms.

Tears running down his lined cheeks, Simeon clasped the child and sang in a strong, triumphant voice that belied his age, "Lord, now lettest thou thy servant depart in peace, according to thy word: for mine eyes have seen thy salvation, which thou hast prepared before the face of all people; a light to lighten the Gentiles, and the glory of thy people Israel" (Luke 2:29-32). This great hymn of assurance has formed part of the daily prayers of the Church since the fourth century. We can enter into the amazement, joy, and fulfillment Simeon must have felt as we pray with his words.

The Song of Simeon has become known as the Nunc Dimittis from its opening Latin words and its theme: "Now let thy servant depart in peace." Simeon had touched Christ, he had experienced salvation—what more could he ask of this life? William Barclay recounts that in contrast to the majority of Jews of that time, there were a few who were known as *the quiet in the land.* They had not put their faith in armies and earthly kingdoms, but in constant prayer and quiet watchfulness for God's coming. Simeon was one of the quiet ones, "In humble and faithful expectation he was waiting for the day when God would comfort his people."[1]

In verses 34 and 35 Simeon continues his prophecy by warning that by Christ many would fall, many would rise, and hearts would be revealed. Simeon's own heart was revealed in his song, and his response to the goodness and loveliness of Christ serves as a model for us all. But, as Barclay warns, if a person, "when so confronted, remains coldly unmoved or actively hostile, he is condemned. . . . Towards Jesus Christ there can be no neutrality. We either surrender to him or are at war with him. And it is the tragedy of life that our pride often keeps us from making that surrender which leads to victory."[2]

Prayer Guide
Praying for the Light to Shine

1. Read Matt. 2:1-12. *Epiphany* means "appearance": the appearance of God on earth, the appearance of the star in the sky, the appearance of the wise men at the manger. In what ways has God appeared to you?

2. God led the wise men to Christ with the star; He led Simeon to the Temple by His Holy Spirit. Read Luke 2:25-35. How have you known His leading? Recount a specific story.

3. Our study of Advent was about waiting for a promise. This week we saw Simeon waiting for fulfillment. What do you wait for? How does seeing such waiting satisfied in Scripture help you?

4. Simeon praised God that he had seen His salvation. Are there ways in which you have seen the salvation of the Lord?

5. After Simeon sang his great hymn, he gave Mary and Joseph a blessing and then gave them some solemn warnings. Have you found that God's blessings are sometimes accompanied by trials? Recount a story.

6. One thing that has been promised to all Christians is the future joy of worshiping around the great white throne. The Book of Revelation contains many beautiful songs that we shall sing when we behold Him in heaven as Simeon did on earth. Read Rev. 4:11; 5:9, 12, 13b; 11:17; 12:10-12a; 15:3-4; 19:1-17. Record some of your favorite praises.

7. Write a prayer in your journal, praising God for the work of Christ as Simeon did.

8. Pray both your prayer and Simeon's as a conclusion to your regular devotions each day this week.

Notes

Introduction

1. Robert Webber, *Worship Old and New* (Grand Rapids: Zondervan, 1994), 226.
2. Ibid.
3. Ibid.

Chapter 1

1. John Wesley, "Journal" in *Works* 1:485.
2. *Book of Common Prayer* (New York: Church Hymnal Corp., 1979).
3. Dallas Willard, *The Divine Conspiracy* (San Francisco: Harper San Francisco, 1998), 269.
4. Charles Simeon, *Expository Outlines on the Whole Bible* (Grand Rapids: Zondervan, 1955) 11:205.

Chapter 3

1. John Wesley, *Explanatory Notes upon the New Testament* (London: Epworth Press, 1977), 37.

Chapter 4

1. Turgot, *Life of St. Margaret*, published as *Saint Margaret* (Edinburgh: Floris Books, 1993).
2. Wesley, "Journal" in *Works* 1:260.
3. Ibid., 309.
4. Ibid., 3:307.
5. Ibid., "Sermons on Several Occasions" in *Works* 5:135.
6. Wesley, *Explanatory Notes upon the New Testament*, 38.

Chapter 6

1. Simeon, *Expository Outlines* 11:199-203. Adapted in Donna Fletcher Crow, *To Be Worthy* (Wheaton, Ill.: Crossway Books, 1995), 67-70.

Chapter 7

1. Gabriele Lusser Rico, *Writing the Natural Way* (Los Angeles: J. P. Tarcher, 1983), 118.
2. Simeon, *Expository Outlines*, 203.
3. Ibid., 205.
4. Wesley, *Explanatory Notes upon the New Testament*, 38.

Chapter 8

1. Robert Webber, *Rediscovering the Christian Feasts* (Peabody, Mass.: Hendrickson Publishers, 1998), 49.
2. Thomas Merton, *Praying the Psalms* (Collegeville, Minn.: Liturgical Press, 1956), 7.
3. Ibid.
4. Ibid., 8.
5. Ibid., 9.
6. Ibid., 44.

7. Ibid., 39.

Chapter 9

1. Webber, *Rediscovering the Christian Feasts,* 66.
2. Wesley, "Journal" in *Works* 2:527.
3. Webber, *Rediscovering the Christian Feasts,* 66.
4. *Beacon Bible Commentary* (Kansas City: Beacon Hill Press of Kansas City, 1967), 3:433.

Chapter 10

1. *Explanatory Notes upon the Old Testament* (Salem, Ohio: Schmul Publishers, 1975), 2:1055.
2. Simeon, *Expository Outlines* 5:128.
3. *Beacon Bible Commentary* 3:188.

Chapter 11

1. John Wesley, *Works,* "Letter to the Rev. Mr. Bailey of Core," 1750.
2. Simeon, *Expository Outlines* 6:419-20.

Chapter 12

1. Wesley, *Works* 4:70.
2. Ibid., 95.
3. Ibid., 223.
4. Ibid., 270.
5. Ibid., 484.
6. *Book of Common Prayer,* 170-71.
7. *Beacon Bible Commentary* 3:212.
8. *Book of Common Prayer,* 288.

Chapter 13

1. Robert E. Webber, ed., *Services of the Christian Year,* vol. 5 in *The Complete Library of Christian Worship* (Peabody, Mass.: Hendrickson Publishers, 1993), 427.
5. Evelyn Birge Vitz, *A Continual Feast* (San Francisco: Ignatius Press, 1985), 211.
6. Wesley, *Works* 7:509.

Chapter 14

1. Wesley, *Works* 6:254.
2. Ibid., 7:425.
3. Ibid., 5:22.
4. Ibid., 167.

Chapter 15

1. Wesley, *Works,* "A Plain Account of Christian Perfection," 11:438.
2. Quoted in Dom Gregory Dix, *The Image and Likeness of God* (Westminster: Dacre Press), 63.
3. Ibid.
4. Ibid., 64.
5. Brother Lawrence, *The Practice of the Presence of God* (New York: Doubleday, 1977), 99.
6. Ibid., Foreword, 9.
7. Ibid., 12.

8. Ibid., 56.

9. Ibid., 75.

10. Ron DelBene, *The Breath of Life* (Nashville: Upper Room Books, 1992), 19.

11. Evelyn Underhill, *Concerning the Inner Life,* quoted in ibid., 69 (emphasis added).

12. *The Cloud of Unknowing,* quoted in DelBene, *Breath of Life,* 77.

Chapter 16

1. John Bunyan, *Pilgrim's Progress* (Philadelphia: John C. Winston Co., 1993), 167-68.

2. Wesley, *Works* 5:387.

3. Lawrence, *Practice of the Presence of God,* 77.

4. C. S. Lewis, *Letters to Malcolm: Chiefly on Prayer* (New York: Harcourt Brace and Co., 1964), 11.

5. Ibid.

6. Francis de Sales, *Introduction to the Devout Life,* trans. John Ryan (New York: Doubleday, 1966), 84.

7. Thomas Keating, *Intimacy with God* (New York: Crossroad Publishing Co., 1998), 9.

8. Ibid., 41.

9. William Johnston, ed., *The Cloud of Unknowing* (New York: Doubleday, 1973), 56.

10. Ibid., 60.

Chapter 17

1. Wesley, *Works* 5:54.

2. Esther De Waal, *Seeking God: The Way of St. Benedict* (Collegeville, Minn.: Liturgical Press, 1984), 145.

3. Ibid., 146.

Chapter 18

1. Matthew Henry, *Commentary on the Whole Bible,* New Modern Edition, electronic database (Peabody, Mass.: Hendrickson Publishers, 1991), n.p.

Chapter 19

1. *Nelson's Illustrated Bible Dictionary* (Thomas Nelson, 1986) in *PC Study Bible for Windows* V3.0 (Biblesoft).

Chapter 20

1. Webber, ed. *Services of the Christian Year,* 111.

Chapter 21

1. Henry, *Commentary on the Whole Bible,* n.p.

2. Ibid.

Chapter 22

1. Wesley, *Explanatory Notes upon the New Testament,* 204.

Chapter 23

1. William Barclay, *The Gospel of Luke,* rev. ed. (Philadelphia: Westminster Press, 1975), 26.

2. Ibid., 27.

Glossary

Advent—The ecclesiastical season immediately before Christmas. It includes four Sundays before Christmas Day.

Alb—Long, white robe.

Ash Wednesday—The first day of Lent, six and a half weeks before Easter.

Augustine—(1) of Hippo (354-430), one of the most influential theologians of the church; (2) of Canterbury (d. approx. 609), missionary to England, first Archbishop of Canterbury.

Barclay, William (1907-78)—Scottish New Testament scholar, known for his *Daily Study Bible.*

Book of Common Prayer—The official service book of the Anglican Church since 1549.

Canticle—Song based on biblical text such as Mary's Magnificat and Simeon's Nunc Dimittis.

Didache—A first-century manual on Christian morals and Church practice.

Doxology—A hymn of praise to the Persons of the Trinity.

Eastertide—The seven weeks from Easter until Pentecost Sunday.

Epiphany—Feast of the Church on January 6, the 12th day of Christmas.

Eucharist (Thanksgiving)—The Lord's Supper.

Fathers of the Church—A group of writers from the Early Church whose authority on doctrinal matters carry special weight. This group includes: Hippolytus (170-236), Tertullian (160-225), and Irenaeus (130-200).

Festoon—Chain of flowers, ribbon, and so forth, hung as adornment.

Flex—In chant, to change pitch.

Great Triduum—The three last days of Holy Week commemorating the Last Supper, Passion, and Death of Christ.

Henry, Matthew (1662—1714)—Nonconformist biblical exegete, known primarily for his exposition of the Old and New Testaments.

Holy Week—The week preceding Easter.

Holy Club—Nickname given to the group of Methodists that John Wesley formed at Oxford in 1729.

Kyrie Eleison—Part of the ordinary, a prayer for divine mercy, "Lord, have mercy."

Lectio Divina—"Divine Reading" or reading Scripture as a form of prayer.

Lent—The period of spiritual preparation 40 days before Easter.

Leonine Sacramentary—A book of prayers from the fifth century.

Liturgy—Fixed form of public worship.

Matins—Morning prayer.

Maundy Thursday—Thursday of Holy Week, focusing on John 13:34.

Nave—The long body of a church.

Nicene Creed—Statement of faith issued in 325 by the Council of Nicaea to defend against the Arian heresy.

Ordinary—The historic order of a church service that does not vary with the seasons.

Paschal—Easter.

Pentecost—Jewish Feast of Weeks, the day the Holy Spirit descended on the apostles, celebrated as the birthday of the Church.

Sanctus—Hymn of praise that is part of the ordinary. "Holy, holy, holy" (Isa. 6:3).

Sarum Missal—Order of worship followed in the Cathedral of Salisbury in medieval times.

Simeon, Charles (1759—1836)—Fellow of King's College, Cambridge, leader of Evangelical Revival.

Tenebrae (darkness)—A Holy Week service in which the lights are extinguished.

Teresa—(1) Saint of Avila (1515-82), an important writer on the life of prayer; (2) Mother, of Calcutta (1910-98), founded Sisters of Charity.

The Cloud of Unknowing—A 14th-century book on contemplative prayer by an anonymous English writer.

Vigil—To keep watch or pray, especially on the eve of a festival.

Webber, Robert—Professor of theology, Wheaton College, director of Institute for Worship Studies.

Wesley, John (1703-91)—Founder of the Methodist Movement.

Wesley, Charles (1707-88)—Most gifted and prolific of English hymn writers. He composed over 6,000 hymns.

Whitsunday—English name for Pentecost, from the habit of wearing white on that day, although red is most often worn today.

Bibliography

Barclay, William. *The Daily Study Bible Series*, rev. ed., *The Gospel of Luke, The Gospel of John*, vol. 2, *The Gospel of Matthew*, vols. 1 and 2, 1975. Philadelphia: Westminster Press.

Beacon Bible Commentary, vols. 3, 6, 7, and 8. Kansas City: Beacon Hill Press of Kansas City, 1967, 1964, 1965, 1968.

Book of Common Prayer, 1979. New York: Church Hymnal Corporation.

Clarke, W. K. Lowther, ed. *Liturgy and Worship*. London: S.P.C.K., 1954.

Cross, F. L., E. A. Livingstone, eds. *The Oxford Dictionary of the Christian Church*. Oxford: Oxford University Press, 1997.

de Sales, St. Francis. *Introduction to the Devout Life*. Trans. John Ryan. New York: Doubleday, 1966.

De Waal, Esther. *Seeking God: The Way of St. Benedict*. Collegeville, Minn.: Liturgical Press, 1984.

DelBene, Ron. *The Breath of Life, a Simple Way to Pray*. Nashville: Upper Room Books, 1992.

Dix, Dom Gregory. *The Image and Likeness of God*. London: Westminster Dacre Press, 1953.

Dubruiel, Michael, and Amy Welborn. *The Biblical Way of the Cross*. Notre Dame, Ind.: Ave Maria Press, 1994.

The Gospel According to St. Luke and *The Gospel According to St. John, Tyndale New Testament Commentaries*. Grand Rapids: William B. Eerdmans Publishing Co., 1977.

Henry, Matthew. *Commentary on the Whole Bible*, New Modern Edition, electronic database. Peabody, Mass.: Hendrickson Publishers, 1991.

Hickman, Saliers, Stookey, and White. *The New Handbook of the Christian Year*. Nashville: Abingdon Press, 1992.

Johnston, William, ed. *The Cloud of Unknowing*. New York: Doubleday, 1973.

Jones, Cheslyn, and Geoffrey Wainwright, eds. *The Study of Liturgy*. New York: Oxford University Press, 1978.

Keating, Thomas. *Intimacy with God*. New York: Crossroad Publishing Co., 1998.

Lawrence, Brother. *The Practice of the Presence of God*. New York: Doubleday, 1977.

Lewis, C. S. *Letters to Malcolm: Chiefly on Prayer*. New York: Harcourt Brace Jovanovich, 1988.

Maskell, William. *The Ancient Liturgy of the Church of England*. London: William Pickering, 1844.

Merton, Thomas. *Contemplative Prayer*. New York: Doubleday, 1989.

————. *Praying the Psalms*. Collegeville, Minn.: Liturgical Press, 1956.

Nelson's Illustrated Bible Dictionary on Biblesoft, PC Study Bible for Windows, Reference Library Edition, Ver. 2.1. Nashville: Thomas Nelson, 1986.

Rico, Gabriele Lusser. *Writing the Natural Way*. Los Angeles: J. P. Tarcher, 1983.

Savin, Olga, trans. *The Way of the Pilgrim*. Boston: Shambala Press, 1991.

Simeon, Charles. *Expository Outlines on the Whole Bible*, 21 vols. Grand Rapids: Zondervan, 1955.

Sing to the Lord, Church of the Nazarene Hymnal. Kansas City: Lillenas Publishing Co., 1993.

Turgot, *Saint Margaret,* ed. Iain MacDonald. Edinburgh: Floris Books, 1993.

Veith, Gene Edward, Jr. *Reading Between the Lines.* Wheaton, Ill.: Crossway Books, 1990.

Vitz, Evelyn Birge. *A Continual Feast.* San Francisco: Ignatius Press, 1985.

Webber, Robert E., ed. *The Services of the Christian Year,* vol. 5, *The Complete Library of Christian Worship.* Peabody, Mass.: Hendrickson Publishers, 1993.

————. *Worship Old and New.* Grand Rapids: Zondervan, 1994.

Wesley, John. *Explanatory Notes upon the New Testament.* London: Epworth Press, 1977.

————. *Explanatory Notes upon the Old Testament,* vol. 2. Salem, Ohio: Schmul Publishers, 1975.

————. "Letter to Mr. Bailey of Core," "The Mystery of Iniquity," "On Grieving the Holy Spirit," "On Laying the Foundation of the New Chapel," "The Almost Christian," "The Repentance of Believers," *The Works of John Wesley,* on compact disc. Franklin, Tenn.: Providence House Publishers, 1995.

————. "Journal," *The Works of John Wesley,* vol. 1. Grand Rapids: Zondervan, n.d.

————. "Sermons on Several Occasions," *The Works of John Wesley,* vol. 5. Grand Rapids: Zondervan, n.d.

Willard, Dallas. *The Divine Conspiracy.* San Francisco: Harper San Francisco, 1998.

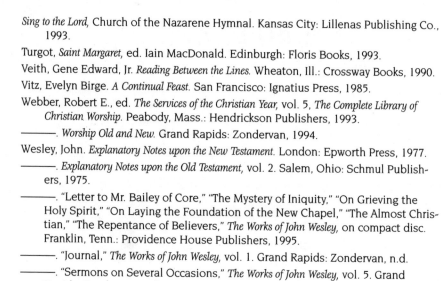

If you are interested in

Small-Group Applications

for *Seasons of Prayer,*

please contact

Beacon Hill Press of Kansas City

P.O. Box 419527

Kansas City, MO 64141

816-931-1900

Fax: 816-753-4071

or E-mail: inquiry@bhillkc.com